ON THE THIRTY NINE ARTICLES

A Conversation with Tudor Christianity

ON THE THIRTY NINE ARTICLES

A Conversation with Tudor Christianity

OLIVER O'DONOVAN

Published for Latimer House, Oxford
by
THE PATERNOSTER PRESS
EXETER

AUSTRALIA:
Bookhouse Australia Ltd.,
P.O. Box 115, Flemington Markets, NSW 2129

SOUTH AFRICA:
Oxford University Press,
P.O. Box 1141, Cape Town

A Latimer Monograph

Latimer House, Oxford, is a centre for study and research. It is committed to
the life of creatively applying biblical and reformed theology to the ongoing life
of the Church of England and the Anglican Communion. This book is one
of a series of occasional studies on theological subjects sponsored by the
Latimer House Council, which bear on issues of importance for Anglicans.

British Library Cataloguing in Publication Data

O'Donovan, Oliver
    On the 39 articles : a conversation with Tudor
Christianity.
    1. Church of England—Articles of religion
    I. Title
    238'.342   BX5137

ISBN 0-85364-435-7

Photoset in Great Britain by
Busby Typesetting & Design, Exeter, Devon,
and printed for the Paternoster Press,
Paternoster House, 3 Mount Radford Crescent, Exeter, Devon,
by A. Wheaton & Co., Ltd., Exeter, U.K.

CONTENTS

INTRODUCTION

What excuses can I make to the reader of theological books for asking him to entertain, in this "conversation" with Tudor Christianity, a rather self-indulgent undertaking? It is evident to myself, and will be more so to others, that I have no qualifications to write a historical work about the sixteenth century church; while such credit as I might have as a theologian will quickly be dispelled, it must seem, by my grave lack of seriousness — I having it in mind neither to raise disturbing questions about faith for someone else to answer, nor to reflect inconclusively on a multitude of theological methodologies, nor even to "reconstruct" theology by way of a new synthesis with the social sciences! I am driven back upon the lame defence that this is the kind of enterprise which theologians ought from time to time to set their hands to.

It is intended as a *conversation* with a Christian text from the past, the Thirty Nine Articles of the Church of England. It is not a *study* of that text, for that would imply that the text itself had become the sole objection of attention. In conducting a study the scholar puts his intellectual powers completely at the service of the text, and makes it his only business to enable the text to speak clearly. It is a weakness in his work if his own concerns and the fashions of his time intrude. What I propose in this case, however, is not to talk solely about the Articles, but the talk about God, mankind and redemption, the central matters of the Christian faith, and to take the Tudor authors with me as companions in discussion. Two voices will be speaking, a late modern and an early modern one, discussing (as equal partners, we shall hope) matters of concern to both, each raising the questions that Christian faith in his time forces upon him.

Surprisingly enough, this is a type of discussion which is not too frequently undertaken. Surprisingly, because it is the paradigm of what our theologians of the late twentieth century, who are not lacking in a sense of their duty to "the tradition", most commonly see themselves as doing. And it would be hard to devise a better discipline for them than such a conversation affords: to develop their thoughts in sustained response to the thinkers of another age, accepting the others' priorities and answering their questions, interpreting the others' views and developing the modern perspective in counterpoint to them, all the time restraining themselves, as good conversationalists, from haranguing God and man with the urgent preoccupations of their own day. Yet it has its disadvantages too. Tact forbids the participant in such a dialogue to develop the modern questions as extensively as they demand; nor is he free to turn away from his chosen companions to take up points of interest with his coevals. It is best undertaken, then, as a propaedeutic exercise, a preliminary to the more elevated and demanding tasks of theology. And it is best approached in a comparatively relaxed way, not in the academical full dress of the Schools but informally beside the fireplace — yet never forgetting that if (as we are told) evil conversation corrupteth good manners, so bad academic manners can also corrupt good conversation.

We have taken for our partner in this conversation the kind of theological text that is most suited for it, a church document intended to exercise a normative role as a standard of belief in its community. The very features which make such a text less interesting to read than the work of a major individual thinker, make it more rewarding to have a discussion with. It is brief. It invites elaboration, providing a skeletal structure which its readers may cover with the flesh and blood of their own argumentation. It purports to speak for a whole community, and to say only that which the community can and must say together. It intends to confine itself to the most important things. A conversation with Tudor Christianity requires a text that is, in a strong sense, representative. When we engage with the Articles we engage with a whole community, and not with an individual genius (for even Cranmer does not speak simply for himself), the peculiarities of whose outlook, the waywardness or compellingness of whose arguments, the distinctiveness of whose position vis a vis his contemporaries, may quite possibly leave us absorbed in the sheer task of exegesis and put to silence in respectful admiration. This is not to doubt that we may *learn* infinitely more by waiting upon the great thinkers; but we *develop ourselves* in certain ways by venturing upon discussion with the church document that speaks for the whole age.

But we must acknowledge an objection which will be raised against any discussion with the Articles, especially when the modern partner is an Anglican theologian. Is it fitting, in an age striving for ecumenical advance, that we should pursue our theological concerns in such a narrowly sectarian fashion? The Articles, together with the Book of Common Prayer, are the foundation of Anglican theology. What status has *Anglican* theology as such, when we have admitted, in principle at least, the common task of living and thinking together as Christians? And why should further currency be given to a polemical document when all our efforts are devoted to overcoming these traditional polemics? Such an objection has, to my mind, a *prima facie* validity; and I would not be prepared merely to brazen out the charge of being an ecumenical reactionary. Let me try to answer it autobiographically, giving the reader at the same time some idea of how this book came to birth.

When I began teaching theology at an English college some years ago, I would have reacted to the idea that I should use this document as a text for instruction with frank distaste. We still lived under the shadow of the old party controversies which had raged about the Articles for a hundred years or more because of the requirement of subscription by candidates for ordination. We were trying, if anything, to wean our students away from the old handbooks on the Articles which had provided the staple doctrinal teaching for the previous generation of clergymen. They were conceived as manuals for induction into a party tradition, comfortably reassuring about what it was permissible for an Anglican parson of the right persuasion to believe, uncomfortably challenging to the doubtful convictions of the other party. They inculcated minute scholarship on details, disagreeable prejudices on generalities. The picture that they gave of the Articles was lopsided, preoccupied by the polemical concerns of the late Victorian age. On such modes of instruction we turned our backs with sighs of relief (too fulsome, perhaps) and congratulated ourselves on rediscovering what the true task of theology ought to be: to respond to the intellectual and spiritual challenges of our day under the tutelage and authority of Scripture alone.

But in England we were all Anglicans without trying to be. When I moved to Toronto and began to teach Canadians from a minority Anglican church in an overtly ecumenical context, I discovered to my dismay that I could not communicate what seemed to me self-evident universal priorities to students who were searching for a sense of denominational identity. It became clear to me that if nobody offered them a theological understanding of what it was to be an Anglican, they would look for their Anglican identity in the most foolish and untheological places, never discovering, perhaps, that being an Anglican was nothing other than a mode of being a Christian. And so

I learned what ought to have been an elementary lesson — that our universal communion in the truth of the gospel will not come about by the denial of denominational traditions, but only by the critical appropriation and sharing of them. I think I was not deceiving myself when I observed that my Canadian Anglican students began to make an altogether more confident use of the ecumenical resources of their School when they had first been introduced to what Tudor Anglicans understood the essential truth of the gospel to be. But to assure ecumenical good faith, and to quieten a nagging scruple that I might be guilty of purely polemical indoctrination, I added to my course on the Articles on the last occasion that I taught it a new feature, which quite transformed it. Promising (with some trepidation) not to alter a word to accommodate him, I invited my friend Dr. George Schner S.J. to attend the course throughout, and gave him an opportunity at each meeting of the class to comment from a Roman Catholic perspective on how we Anglicans were presenting ourselves in the eyes of our fellow-Christians. I can only wish it were practicable to incorporate some such feature into a book; for thanks to Dr. Schner's sensitivity and acuteness, we were all helped to see how, in reaching to recover our Anglican tradition, we were being led into areas of theological concern that we held in common with those whom we would once have identified as our opponents. It is in the same spirit, and hoping for the same sort of result, that I dare to put our conversations with the Articles, somewhat revised, into public circulation.

For the benefit of those who used to know but have forgotten, it may be as well to rehearse very briefly the origins of the English Articles of Religion as we now have them. ("We" here refers to all Anglican churches except for the Episcopal Church of America, which produced a conservative revision to meet its changed circumstances in 1801). They went through two recensions, the earlier appearing at the end of the reign of Edward VI (1553), the later at the beginning of Elizabeth's reign. The Elizabethan Articles themselves appeared in two versions, one in Latin (1563) and the other in English (1571). The differences between the two Elizabethan versions are not of great moment. Nervousness about Catholic-leaning sentiment led to the withdrawal of one Article (29) in 1563, which was restored in 1571. Apart from this discrepancy, we can treat the two versions simply as the Latin and English texts of the one document, the English not quite a straight translation of the Latin.

The Elizabethan Articles are a careful and thorough revision, undertaken by Matthew Parker with the assistance of other bishops, and then further amended in Convocation, of the forty two Articles which had been prepared by Thomas Cranmer (in both Latin and English) on the eve of the Marian crisis. Cranmer is, in effect, the "author" of our Thirty Nine Articles; for although Parker's revisions were extensive, especially in the second half of the document, Cranmer's conception and order was preserved, and his theological personality continued to give the Articles their distinctive character. The revisers were cautious and tidy. They filled gaps that Cranmer had left (with an Article on the Holy Spirit (5), on good works (12), and with two (29, 30) on the eucharist); they removed what they thought to be unnecessary or tendentious Articles (10 on the Edwardian list, on grace; 16 on blasphemy against the Holy Spirit, and four (39-42) on the Last Things); they tidied away one which they thought out of place (19, on the commandments of the law, incorporated into 7). They edited, corrected, sometimes rewrote. They made the Articles into a better document for church use; but to compare the two recensions is to see how the flash of theological imagination was always Cranmer's.

The revisers had before them the so-called Confession of Würtemberg, a submission by Lutheran delegates to the Council of Trent, and it has been observed that this document influenced the Elizabethan revisions at various points, though hardly to the extent of a sustained quotation. More importantly, the famous Augsburg Confession had provided a form of words for some passages in the Articles of God and Christ (1, 2), on justification (11) and on the church (19). This Confession had formed the basis for thirteen unratified articles of agreement between Lutheran theologians and the English Church in 1538, a part of Thomas Cromwell's ill-fated attempt to lead Henry VIII into alliance with the German princes, and Cranmer made use of those articles in drafting his own. These two influences are responsible for an occasional Lutheran flavour, which is, however, no greater than one would expect, given the influence of Luther upon the early Reformation as a whole. At points where Lutheranism distinguished itself from the other traditions of the Reformation, notably in its doctrine of the eucharist, the English Articles show no Lutheran leanings. As for the famous tag about the Church of England having Calvinist Articles, that rests upon an anachronistic reading of Article 17.

It is not only the ecumenical question that might cause us to hesitate before embarking on a conversation with the Articles. We may expect quizzical looks, too, from those who doubt whether anything of importance about the Anglican doctrinal tradition can be learned from *this* source.

It is certainly true that Protestant Anglicans who have championed the Articles have sometimes made claims for their role as a norm of Anglican belief which are too extensive. This has sprung from a desire to interpret the Anglican church as a church of the Reformation, based, like other Reformation churches, upon a great Confession. But although the Anglican church is indeed a church of the Reformation, it does not relate to its Reformation origins in quite the same way as other churches do, and its Articles are not exactly comparable, in their conception or in the way they have been used, to the Augsburg or Westminster Confessions or to the Heidelberg Catechism. It is not simply that they are supposed to be read in conjunction with the Book of Common Prayer. There is a more important difference, which is that the Anglican doctrinal tradition, born of an attempt (neither wholly successful nor wholly unsuccessful) to achieve comprehensiveness within the limits of a Christianity both catholic and reformed, is not susceptible to the kind of textual definition which the Confessions (on the Protestant side) and the conciliar decrees (on the Catholic) afford. One might almost say that Anglicans have taken the authority of the Scriptures and the Catholic creeds too seriously to be comfortable with another single doctrinal norm.

Nevertheless, it is absurd to suggest that there is simply no immediate authority for doctrine in the Anglican churches — though the delusion does fall from time to time upon distracted prelates that the Anglican tradition is defined by what they think it is! It is rather that authority is, as we sometimes say, "diffused". And of all the places to which it is diffused, the documents of the Tudor settlement (Articles and Prayer Book — the Books of Homilies have hardly achieved the significance that was intended for them) are certainly the most important. That is not offered as a purely normative judgment, but also as a descriptive one. The Tudor church has exercised the most profoundly formative role in determining what Anglicanism ever since, in all its varieties, has been and now is. Each century has left its stamp on us; but the sixteenth has determined the shape of the whole.

In that century English Christians had heard some of the most important things that Northern Europe as a whole had heard from the word of God. Yet ought we rather to say that they had *overheard* them? Look at the shape of the Articles: eighteen on God, man and salvation, twenty one on the "visible" church, its institutions, its relation to government and its sacraments! Do we not say, "Here is the church of Laud, of the Lambeth Quadrilateral, of the 1928 Prayer Book controversy, already declaring itself! A church concentrating, in defiance of all that Luther would have told it, upon maintaining the external forms of religion!"? But that would be one-sided and hasty. It would be truer to say that it was not then, and has never been to this day, the genius of the Church of England to grow its own theological nourishment, but only to prepare what was provided from elsewhere and to set it decently upon the table. But in that early period this minor genius actually served its purpose. The nourishment it brought in from Europe was good; the preparation was judicious, and the service never more decent. The English Reformation supported a Christian culture — a factor that is too easily overlooked when we turn our attention to the narrowly ecclesiastical concerns of the period. Shakespeare and Spenser flourished in its ethos; Herbert and Donne (in a later reign, but before the great sea-change of the seventeenth century) grew up in its wake. *The Merchant of Venice* and *The Faerie Queene* also provide evidence for the theological health of the Elizabethan age, just as *Paradise Lost* does for the Puritan.

There is, in truth, a great gulf between the preoccupations of the sixteenth and of the seventeenth centuries — so great that one could almost, at a pinch, claim the Reformation as the last great flowering of the mediaeval era and the seventeenth century as the moment at which the modern broke in. Of course, it is more complicated than that; already in the Reformation we find ourselves peering across the threshold of modernity. Nevertheless, such a claim would be no more misleading, and perhaps rather less, than the view which conceives of the Reformation as a radical announcement of the supremacy of the individual conscience. The Reformers were concerned especially with the mediaeval question of justification, which they reinterpreted radically in a Christocentric way. From the seventeenth century on, this question sinks out of sight in the English-speaking tradition like a stone in a deep pond. In its place we find new questions about individual human agency and natural causes, transforming theology, natural philosophy and political theory out of all recognition. The early seventeenth-century preoccupation with predestination, represented in Anglicanism by the unofficial Lambeth Articles of 1595 and the Church of Ireland Articles of 1615, forms a bridge between the two quite different intellectual eras. For predestination, itself a mediaeval issue, proved a natural way of approaching newly-urgent questions about causation and agency in terms which were familiar. But we must not read our Tudor authors as though they were the conscious harbingers of this intellectual revolution. Cranmer's seventeenth Article is not an early draft for the work of Whitgift and Ussher. One of the services which Cranmer and his contemporaries may render us, us late-moderns whose conceptions have been shaped by the maturing of that liberal-scientific culture which was born in the seventeenth century, is to take us behind it, back to a time when other questions, closer to the centre of Christian proclamation, took priority.

We will learn from them better than from Anglicans of any other age of that distinctive theological virtue in which Anglicans have sometimes spoken as though they had a monopoly, the virtue of "moderation". The word is appropriate enough, though it needs to be used with some subtlety and not a little irony. The popular account of

Anglican moderation, that it consisted in steering a steady middle path between the exaggerated positions of Rome on the one hand and Geneva on the other, simply will not bear examination. As our knowledge of late-mediaeval thought grows greater, forwarded by the scholarly studies of the last half-century, it becomes more apparent that Calvinism, on all issues except that of church-order, took as much of the late-scholastic tradition into its system as any of the other schools of Protestantism. Its doctrine of predestination can arguably claim to be less "reformed" — in the sense of bring more mediaeval — than that of the Council of Trent! There was nothing particularly "middle" about most of the English Reformers' theological positions — even if one could decide between what poles the middle way was supposed to lie.

Their moderation consisted rather in a determined policy of separating the essentials of faith and order from adiaphora. Of all the continental spirits, they had learned most deeply, perhaps, from Melanchthon. "Surely odious it must have been," Hooker exclaims, "for one Christian church to abolish that which all had received and held for the space of many ages, and that without detriment unto religion so manifest and so great, as might in the eyes of unpartial men appear sufficient to clear them from all blame of rash and inconsiderate proceeding, if in fervour of zeal they had removed such things."[1] Anglican moderation is the policy of reserving strong statement and conviction for the few things which really deserve them. Yet that does not mean that it is incapable of conveying certainties. Think of the church music of the Tudor period, after its composers had turned over to English and put away their soaring cloud-peaks of polyphonic sonority. It moves along at a deliberate, purposeful walking-pace — not dancing like Purcell, not clapping its hands like Handel, not swelling its breast like Stanford. It articulates its text clearly in cool and measured understatement, without embellishment. It conveys confidence and assurance; and it can even suggest excitement, though under the strongest self-restraint.

The moderation of Anglicanism has proved invaluable in those heady moments of the history of the modern church at which truth has broken, with shocking suddenness, upon the whole culture. But it can also be treacherous when the culture is drifting without truth and without certainty. We may compare it with the secular English conservatism of our own century. Far from being a refusal of change, English conservatism is rather a way of excusing it, by maintaining the pretence that change has simply been forced upon it. Scrupulously preserving apparent continuity in everything inessential, it manages to

[1] *Laws of Ecclesiastical Polity* IV.14.6.

dissimulate altogether the profundity of the revolution that has overwhelmed it. The Anglican genius, similarly, is not sufficient on its own to provide a strong sense of direction, but depends upon the guidance of other Christians' dreams and visions. But it is precisely that, and not some supposed "middleness" between Catholic and Protestant, which gives it a critically important role in twentieth century ecumenism.

It is none of the Christian theologian's business, in the end, to make great boasts for his denominational tradition or for any era in its history. His task is to bend his mind, under the authority of the apostolic witness to Christ, to the demands of Christian faith and obedience as they confront him and his contemporaries in their own time. If he does that, let him learn from whom he will, as he will. Yet those of us who have learned to follow Jesus Christ here, within the Church of England or one of its sister-churches, have our purely domestic reasons for gratitude. As a token of which I offer this essay to the glory of God and in thanks to those who are responsible for my Christian education as well as to those in England and Canada, whom it has been my privilege to teach. And it is my pleasure to salute the Council and staff of Latimer House on their twenty-fifth anniversary, and especially to thank the Warden, the Revd. Roger Beckwith, for detailed comments which have been of great assistance.

June 28th 1985
Christ Church, Oxford.

1

FAITH IN GOD AND CHRIST
(Articles 1, 2)

The Thirty Nine Articles begin with five articles on the doctrines of the Trinity and the incarnation.

We may observe in the first place a certain perfunctoriness about them. It is not simply that out of thirty nine, five seems few for the basic proclamations of the Christian faith, nor even that these five are, compared with some of the others, on the short side. The suggestion of perfunctoriness is conveyed also by the very traditional way in which they are expressed. The language of the first two and of the fourth is drawn largely from the Augsburg Confession, which was in turn content to use the long-hollowed terminology of the patristic and mediaeval church. The first article of the Augsburg Confession begins: "The churches in our fellowship teach with remarkable unanimity that the decree of the Council of Nicaea about the unity of the divine essence is true and to be believed without doubt." It goes on to condemn Manichaeans, Valentinians, Arians and Eunomians — all of them heresies from the fourth century! The early Reformation wished to appear not only orthodox but also traditional in what it said about God and Christ. In the vast intellectual upheaval of the period there emerged, among other disturbing trends, a renewed Unitarianism. The churches of the early Reformation responded to this simply by aligning themselves with the Catholic tradition. They did no major new theological work on the doctrines of God and Christ.

At the same time, while we may observe how traditional and

perfunctory the first five articles are, we must not miss the significance of the fact that they *are* the first five articles. Even if the English Reformers had nothing new to say about God and Christ, they were not to be discouraged from saying something old. We should be struck by their concern to subordinate the controversial material of the later articles, pressing and urgent as it was, to a restatement of the primitive gospel message. The Church of Ireland Articles of 1615 and the Westminster Confession of 1647, though they deal more fully than the Tudor Articles with the doctrines of God and Christ, nevertheless do not place them first. Following the pattern set by the two Swiss Confessions of 1536 and 1566, they begin with a section on what we would now call theological *method*, the doctrine of revelation and Holy Scripture. It is a defensible order and much more modern in its assumptions; but it is hard not to feel that the Tudor theologians had a true Christian instinct in putting God before method. "There is but one living and true God." Is that not the right way for a Christian to begin stating his faith — however much he may wish, as a theologian, to comment on methodological questions at a later stage? The whole theological undertaking arises from the simple affirmation of a believer: "I believe in God."

God comes first; the revelation of God in Jesus Christ comes second. Again, it could as well have been arranged the other way round. It would be more in the style of the twentieth century to begin with Jesus of Nazareth, and move backwards from him to what he shows us about God. Perhaps Article 1 might have begun, as did Zwingli's Articles of 1523, "The sum of the gospel is, that Christ, the Son of the living God, made known to us the will of his heavenly Father, and that his innocence redeemed us from eternal death and reconciled us to God." In the order of knowledge that sequence is correct. The Christian claims to know what he knows about God, because God has made himself known in Jesus. "No one knows the Father except the Son and any one to whom the Son chooses to reveal him" (Matt. 11:27). But in the order of reality things are the other way round. Jesus does not exist in or for himself. "The Son can do nothing of his own accord, but only what he sees the Father doing; for whatever he does, that the Son does likewise" (Jn. 5:19). There is a priority of the Father to the Son. The Son exists for the Father, and is oriented towards him. For the Anglican Reformers, who were deeply concerned with epistemological questions, reality, nevertheless, was, in the last resort, more important even than knowledge itself.

The article begins by declaring God's unity and transcendence in a series of epithets which owe more to the philosophical vocabulary of Platonism than they do to the vocabulary of the Scriptures. The earliest attempts at explaining and defending the Christian faith were made in an intellectual context dominated by what we normally refer to today as "Middle Platonism", a popular philosophy derived, though at some remove and with other influences, especially Stoic, from the writings of the great Athenian philosopher of the fourth century B.C. Early Christian thinkers found it convenient to use Platonic terminology because it expressed two points about the being of God which they found constantly emphasized in the Old Testament, and especially in the prophets: that God is one, and without rival, and that he far transcends every image, mental or physical, that we may make of him. Christian thinkers pointed out that Platonic philosophers shared the prophets' hostility to crude anthropomorphic ideas of God. The world we know is full of things that come to an end; but God has no end and no beginning, he is "everlasting". The world we know is full of things that are limited spatially by their bodies, of things analysable in terms of their constituent elements, of things subject to other forces than themselves; but God is "without body, parts or passions". The key term is "infinite". We are "finite", limited. God is "infinite", unlimited. Whatever bounds our imagination may put upon God (because we are used to thinking only of things that are bounded in one way or another), those bounds must be removed.

However, that does not mean that all we can do towards speaking of God is to pile up a series of negatives: God is *not* this, *not* that, *not* the other. If this were the case we could think of him only as a mystery, an impenetrable darkness on the edge of our experience of which no knowledge of any kind was possible. But God can be known, not because he is the kind of object that our knowledge can accommodate of itself, but because he has *made* himself known to us by his own will to be communicative. "I do not speak in secret, in realms of darkness, I do not say to the sons of Jacob, 'Look for me in the empty void' " (Isaiah 45:19). Thus we can say more than that God is "infinite". We can say that he is "of infinite power, wisdom and goodness". We can use these terms "power", "wisdom", "goodness' — not, of course, imagining that God is powerful merely like a powerful man, or wise merely like a wise man, or good merely in the way that human beings are good; but, nevertheless, with confidence that these are correct terms through which to approach the reality of God, because God has made himself known to us as the Lord, the one from whom no secret is hidden, the source of all good.

It must be conceded that the negatives create a cool impression, and that our first impression of God is that of distance. Does such a way of presenting God respond adequately to the gospel of God's self-disclosure in Jesus Christ?

We may reply, in the first place, that such assertions, cool as they may be, are not themselves without evangelical implications. It is a commonplace in popular theological discussion that an "abstract theism" is something very different from a vital evangelical message. This opposition has a validity in its proper place, but it can be all too facile. It is clear that the vital evangelical message itself will be gravely weakened unless it makes (in some form or other) the assertions that are made here by the *via negativa*. The gospel tells of a God who shows his love to us in Jesus Christ. But such a tale is idle unless this loving God is the ruler of the universe. To say that God is *one* assures us that the God who shows love to us in Christ is the only God there is, and will not be supplanted by some alien force who was not made known in Christ and does not love us. To say that God is *without body* tells us that the divine love which was locally and particularly circumscribed in the bodily life of Jesus is everywhere, that in meeting the man Jesus we meet the one who is equally accessible to every time and place. To say that God is *without parts* is to deny that he is a product of historical composition, and so susceptible to dissolution: the processes of historical coming-to-be and going-out-of-existence did not produce, and cannot remove, this God who loves us in Jesus. And to say that he is *without passions* means that his purpose cannot be deflected by any force anywhere from the resolve to show us love. Here, too, in these words — whether well expressed or ill — is the gospel that should gladden our hearts and comfort us.

For without the proper tension between the transcendence and the incarnate nearness of God, there can simply be no gospel at all. If anyone finds comfort in asserting, "God is near", "God shares our human weakness and limitations", "God is vulnerable to the same accidents and griefs as we are", this comfort is founded upon its being *God* of whom these things are said. There are, after all, many millions of our fellow human-beings of whom these things are also true; and the consideration of this fact offers us no comfort at all. The power of these assertions depends upon the tension that they embody, and on the wonder that they evoke. They trade on the traditional understanding of the godhead as their subject, that their predicates may strike us with the greater force. To recognize and articulate this tension is the task of theology. To exploit the rhetorical power of these assertions while refusing to allow their presuppositions, is to permit theology to become the slave of pathos.

But our reply must go further. We must satisfy ourselves that the use of these *particular* phrases, these cool, philosophical negatives, conjuring up the distance between God and all created things, does not *detract* from the assertion of God's nearness and care for us in Jesus Christ. And here there are two distinct issues to be considered: first, whether the tradition of speech which the Articles follow is inherently capable of making a strong assertion of the incarnation;

and secondly, whether the Articles themselves, which are merely one example of this tradition, make good use of it and succeed in articulating the Christian faith in salvation.

Modern objectors to the *via negativa* take especial offence at the denial of passion to God. The Stoic concept of impassibility, they maintain, could never express the biblical concept of God present in the sufferings of Jesus Christ. We may usefully ask why this denial in particular sticks so uncomfortably in the throat. Why not object to the denial of body (which might seem to imperil the incarnation) or of parts (which might put the Trinity in question) or of limits (which might cast doubt on Christ's death)? The reason is that the objection speaks from its own philosophical milieu, which bears no closer relationship to biblical Christianity than did the Stoic milieu which first spoke of the divine *apatheia*. It is rooted in the romantic idealism of the nineteenth century, with its claim of infinity and universality for the passionate spirit. If the pre-theological provenance of terms or ideas is, of itself, sufficient to incriminate them in the eyes of Christian believers, then, it would seem, modern objectors to God's impassibility stand in no better case than its ancient defenders. But such an assumption betrays an undialectical literalism of mind; and we should not hesitate to admit that terms and ideas from various philosophical backgrounds may properly serve the theologian in his attempt to speak obediently to the revelation of God in Christ. The question is: what can he do *with* this term or idea? Talk of the negative attributes of God will have to be assessed by its usefulness *in its Christian context*, by the service it renders to those who intend to proclaim God incarnate in the suffering Christ; and not abstractly, by what it might have meant to a non-Christian Stoic, or by what it might irrelevantly suggest to a modern reader unfamiliar with the classical Christian tradition.

Here we may say quite simply that at its best the negative tradition serves theology well, by establishing one pole of the tension between subject and predicate that must be preserved in any statement of the gospel. As an example of this we may give the famous paradox of Athanasius: *apathōs epathen*, "impassibly — he suffered!" It was the impassible Word of God who hung and suffered on the cross, totally identified, through the human nature which he had made his own, with the suffering that belongs to humankind. I do not know how the miracle of God's love can be stated adequately without some such paradox; nor do I see any future in the denial of divine impassibility other than the loss of evangelical tension, and so of the gospel itself. The romantic divinizing of feeling-as-such must tend to replace the message that God became man, with the message that man, by the intensity of his spiritual passionateness, has become god.

This must serve to defend the appropriateness of the negative tradition upon which the Articles draw. As to their own success in using it we need not be too definite, nor rule out differing judgements. Inevitably the reader must allow for their self-imposed role as a summary of essential points, and not expect too much in the way of proclamatory enthusiasm.

There is, however, one observation to be made in their favour, which again has to do with the order in which Cranmer has set out his material. The Articles are unusual among sixteenth-century doctrinal formularies in grouping the treatment of God, Trinity and incarnation together in the early articles. The convention was to put the doctrines of the Trinity at the beginning with the doctrine of God, and then proceed, by way of the creation, fall and original sin, to reach the incarnation in its historical sequence. Both orders are, of course, defensible. The more usual one shows a most creditable concern to treat the incarnation seriously as history; but it tends to leave the doctrine of the Trinity hanging in the air, an appendage to the doctrine of God which must be retained for no particular reason of internal logic. The English order ensures that the statement of God as triune is immediately developed in terms of Jesus of Nazareth. Thus the connexion is strengthened between faith in the Trinity and faith in Christ as saviour. The dry post-Nicene formula of three persons in one substance, pure and eternal, is seen to be pregnant with Christmas, Easter and (though as an afterthought) Pentecost.

The Trinitarian and Christological formulae of the first two articles are the deposit left within the Western church by the Nicene, Constantinopolitan and Chalcedonian Councils of the fourth and fifth centuries, a deposit which ensured (and still ensures, despite mutual suspicions about the way in which these phrases are interpreted) a sense of common Christian faith uniting the churches across the East-West schism, a factor which has been of incalculable importance to the stirrings of ecumenical rapprochement in our own century. Yet Western theologians of our own generation do not read these formulae without at least a slight sense of embarrassment. How much of this embarrassment is justified?

Some of it, no doubt, may be due to the same suspicion of alien philosophical terms which we have already observed in connexion with the negative attributes of transcendence. (We should note, however, that in both Trinitarian and Christological formulae an important part is taken by a word with no pre-history as a technical term in Hellenistic philosophy: *hypostasis*, translated 'person' in the Latin West.) Some of it may be due to the simple fact that these phrases, the product of passionate and profound intellectual searching, have been hardened into definitional formulae, with a normative role for the faith of multitudes who neither wish, nor would be able, to enter into the thinking which produced them. There is an intellectual gauntness about their skeletal structure, so difficult to reclothe with its original flesh and blood; yet it is not an accident of history that these phrases have been held as dogmatic norms, for the Councils, at least, which gave them their authority, intended them for such a role. With these circumstantial difficulties, however, we could live, without too much discomfort. The general sense of unrest which surrounds the Trinitarian and Christological formulae today has deeper roots.

Our thoughts about Christ must conform itself to the *event* of revelation, to what happened as God disclosed himself in Jesus. That event is the subject of the four gospels, which take the form of narratives. This form is not arbitrary or inessential; it is the only correct way to speak of what God has done in Christ, because it is a deed of God, and not simply the being of God, which constitutes the datum of Christology. The four gospels relate the event of divine self-manifestation in the way most appropriate to it. Even of Saint John's Gospel this is true, despite its beginning with a developed announcement of the incarnation of the Word; what the reader is shown (though from the point of view of one who has already foreseen the end) is the event of disclosure as it happened, the triumphing of light over darkness. For theology to comprehend the revelation of God in Christ is to trace and to retrace this disclosure, from before Easter to after it; not, of course, in feigned ignorance of Easter, as though we did not know where the story tended, but allowing Easter to achieve historical depth, as the moment at which God's dealings with Jesus were crowned with completion. There can be no cheating of history, no bypassing of the first dawning of the mystery. Is this to adopt a destructive historicism, which collapses all categories of being and reality into events? We are familiar enough with such a conclusion — but we have no reason to embrace it. It is enough to say that being — *this* being, at any rate, the being of God — is apprehended *through* events which God has set in train, and that theology neither can, nor should wish to, emancipate itself from recapitulating these events, as the creed itself, for all its ontological definiteness, is still prepared to do. If it is true that Jesus *is* the incarnate Word of the Father, it is equally true that thought comes to this acknowledgement through retracing the steps of revelation. Christology, of course, must come to rest in being, and not simply in event; nevertheless, it is itself a train of thought, and not simply a set of conclusions.

This is forced upon us by our reading of the New Testament. The growing dissatisfaction of modern theology with a formal doctrine of God and Christ cast solely in terms derived from the prologue of Saint John's Gospel has been prompted, above all, by the biblical studies of the past century and a half. (Not, of course, that the *formal* doctrine ever comprised the whole of what the Church, which has also an exegetical and homiletic tradition of teaching, had to say on these themes.) Such a strictly Nicene and Chalcedonian framework allowed no room for important biblical categories. We need only think, for example, of how the title "Son of Man" lost its apocalyptic eschatological significance, central to its use in the recorded teaching of Jesus, and was misunderstood as though it represented one half of two-natures doctrine; and of how the title "Son of God" was taken to represent the other half, losing all echoes of the Messianic kingship from which it sprang. Yet this dissatisfaction was really addressed to a restrictive *use* of the Nicene and Chalcedonian formulae, rather than to the formulae themselves. It represented a justified demand that the terms of Christian discussion should be widened to respond to the whole witness of Scripture, not an impugning of these conceptions as such. A fashion in recent years has been to speak of complementary approaches to Christology, "from above" and "from below". The terms are unfortunate in themselves, since they suggest a kind of weighting of our thought to one side or the other of the two-natures doctrine — thus failing to get beyond the Chalcedonian conception on the one hand while treating it entirely arbitrarily on the other! But there is a true perception lying behind them. What ought to be said (and perhaps is really meant by these phrases) is that Christology must grasp the pre-Easter moment together with the post-Easter moment of revelation, and must allow them to interpret each other in a true dialectic, so that our doctrine of Christ achieves its proper historical dimension. Mystery is the disclosure of hiddenness into perspicuity. To speak only in categories of perspicuity distorts and conceals the mystery.

Yet we must speak also in categories of perspicuity; not only of *the appearing of being*, but of *the being which appears*. To refuse this step is to refuse belief in revelation itself, and in Jesus as the disclosure of the Father. If we collapse all being into event, then there is no event of revelation; for revelation is an event which concerns some being which is not itself an event. Perhaps we must say, further, that without being there is no event whatever, but only "process", a movement without reference in reality beyond itself. Certainly, a Christology which is shaped upon the New Testament will find itself required, precisely in order to do justice to the event of God's self-disclosure, to take its stand on the ground of post-Easter perspicuity and to state what it is that has been disclosed. In taking its stand on this ground, it will not have to move one step beyond where the New Testament authors (including the synoptic evangelists) were prepared to stand — though it may make its position more systematically precise than they did. And perhaps it is at this pole of Christological thought that precision and discipline is most necessary, the formulation of normative guidelines most helpful. For it is here, if we are not careful, that undisciplined speculation and fancy can grow wild, where the wilful projection of human abstractions can obscure what God has shown us of himself. It is here, where the incomprehensibility of God is offered to understanding, that we may most easily take flight into cheap dialectic out of a kind of mental panic. Here, then, we need to be directed in careful and ordered terms to what we may say about the being of God and Christ in responsibility to the Scriptures.

And there is always a risk — perhaps a heightened risk, when the depth of Christology is taken seriously, and its force is so much more evident — that we will back away in unbelief. It would be wrong to hide the fact that some of the discomfort which the classical formulae evoke in our age is simply due to our unbelief (in which theologians participate with other Christians, no more and no less), and that what they say, as well as what the New Testament says, has occasionally proved too much for some of us. It may, of course, be that the very way in which theological study has been approached and carried through is so self-consciously determined by scepticism that its conclusion in unbelief, the puzzled shake of the head and the wondering lift of the eyebrow, seems to have been carefully planned from the outset. But who can say that this has always been so? Belief and unbelief are mysterious, just as the relevation itself is a mystery. And in this fact lies our hope, in this unbelieving age, that for any individual or for the church at large the prison-bars may yield at the divine touch — an event which is not itself founded on reason, but is the foundation for reason, just as unbelief is not the conclusion of reason, but the starting point which determines its direction.

Where, then, does unbelief affect us? Curiously (it may seem) not in the statement that God was in Christ — not in that statement *as such*, but in the claim for Christ's pre-existence as the eternal Word of the Father. In comparison with this fundamental stumbling-block for belief, other difficulties (such as with the virgin birth) appear no more than symptomatic. The statement of Christ's pre-existence is, of course, a statement of perspicuity; it belongs to the conclusion, not to the beginning of the event of revelation. For all that it speaks of the beginning *before* the beginning, *that* beginning to the story was not *our* beginning but God's, and so disclosed to us at our end like the divinity of Christ with which it is implicated. Yet it is easier to believe in the divinity of Christ than in his eternal pre-existence. Why?

Because the notion of a God-in-becoming is not uncongenial to the deepest intuitions of humanism, which has applied the attributes of infinity to the process of time and to the history of mankind. Already in the radical monophysitism of the fifth century there was breathed the shocking idea of a "one nature after the union", a new divinized humanity and humanized divinity which, as it were, rendered obsolete the old humanity and divinity which had been known. And out of this Christological seed has sprung much that is modern. A humanity aspiring to transcend itself will feel at home with the paradoxical combination of infinity and innovation. History itself, no longer bounded by the eternal, has taken the eternal into its own changeability by masterful self-transcendence. The Divine Man can as easily be a symbol of this titanic hope as an affront to it. But the Incarnate God, the divinity who has taken humanity into his own unchangeability and is eternally the same — there is a stone of stumbling to the mind shaped by modern historicism, an unmalleable symbol, an uncompromising offence!

2

THE PASSION AND TRIUMPH OF CHRIST
(Articles 2—4)

To expound the story of mankind's redemption in the life, death and resurrection of Jesus is the most weighty task entrusted to theology, and also the hardest. The list of theologians who have done it well is a short one. In the terms set by our own text, we may focus the difficulty like this:- In Articles 2—4 there are five narrative moments which may be singled out within the story: "the Son . . . *took* man's nature in the womb of the blessed Virgin"; he "truly *suffered*, was crucified, dead and buried"; "he *went down* into hell"; he "did truly *arise* again from death"; "he *ascended* into heaven, and there sitteth." How is the theologian to account for this sequence of moments in such a way that they make *one* story of *one* redemption? We are familiar enough with theories of the cross which have no place for Easter, with theologies of resurrection which can make no sense of the ascension, with talk about incarnation which does not need a Paschal Mystery. But good theology should be able to treat of all these moments distinctly, while showing how they are one act of God and not several. In doing so it will also have to distinguish the different ways in which these moments interact with the events of history. For although they make one story of one act, which took place in history under Pontius Pilate, they do not all have identical event-characters. At either end of the sequence there are happenings which have, as it were, one foot in and one foot out of history; they are the beginning and the end of the sacred drama, and beginnings and ends always stand in a strange half-transcendent relation to the events which they bound. In the centre we have a moment which makes the least contact with the time-space of history; and on either side of it, two moments which constitute the Paschal Mystery itself, the death and resurrection of Christ, complementary and equally weighted, to make a genuine *sequence* of events, yet different from each other in the way in which we say that they "happened".

Let us begin at the centre, with the crucifixion and resurrection. From the beginning of the apostolic preaching, these two moments are announced as a *narrative sequence*, linked by the time reference "on the third day", and so complementing one another and constituting a story in themselves, of how God intervened to overthrow death. "This Jesus . . . you crucified and killed . . . But God raised him up . . ." (Acts 2:23f.). And yet it is already clear that these two happenings, differentiated as they are by the human and divine subjects of the verbs, are also different *in kind*. This can be seen in the resurrection-narratives of the gospels, which, though they speak of actual and material happenings, such as the eating of a meal by the lakeside or the touching of healed wounds in the upper room, speak of them mysteriously, as though of a theophany. It is given a thematic development in the contrast made by Saint Paul between the "living body" (*psuchikon*) and the "spiritual body" (*pneumatikon*) (1 Cor. 15:44) and in the distinction made by the First Epistle of Peter between Christ's death "in the flesh" and his coming to life "in the spirit" (1 Pet. 3:18). Theology is here presented with a double temptation. On the one hand it may stress the qualitative difference of the two events to the point where the resurrection ceases to be an event at all within the framework of time and space, or at best is a purely mental event within the disciples' consciousness. This assists the project of unifying the whole, by giving the resurrection a merely noetic or explanatory function, but at the cost of overthrowing the character of redemption as history. The resurrection adds nothing further to the *fact* of the crucifixion, but simply expounds the inner meaning of the crucifixion within God's purposes. Such an approach, essentially gnostic in inspiration, has enjoyed a good deal of favour in the present century. The other temptation, bred of a resistance to gnostic leanings, is so to emphasize the moments as distinct and successive that their intelligible unity is lost sight of; the resurrection becomes the *cancellation* of the crucifixion, the crucifixion nothing more than a work of wicked men which God has cancelled, not something which could happen "according to the definite plan and foreknowledge of God" (Acts 2:23).

Article 4 sets out in resolute fashion to rebut gnostic spiritualizations. Christ "took again his body, with flesh, bones, and all things appertaining to the perfection of man's nature". Do those flesh and bones, we must wonder, protest too loudly? Can the theologian insist so strongly on flesh and bones when he is warned by Saint Paul that flesh and blood cannot inherit the kingdom of God? What he must say, certainly, is that Christ took again his *body*; and that, surely, is the force of the words spoken by the resurrected Christ: "a spirit has not flesh and bones as you see that I have" (Lk. 24:39). Nor need he shrink from the bodily continuity implied in that "again", since the empty tomb is a central element in the gospel narrative. Yet a human body is something more than its material constituents, and what became of those constituents in the resurrection of Jesus's body is a question on which some reticence might be appropriate. It is striking that Cranmer makes so little concession to the words of 1 Pet. 3:18, "made alive in the spirit", a verse which (as we shall shortly see) was in his mind as he drafted these Articles, though it has left no trace on our present text. Is not the difficulty that he could not see how to make concessions to 1 Peter without making concessions to gnosticism — a difficulty shared with some modern gnostics?

But this difficulty arises from a false step which has gone before it: the absolutising of the flesh-spirit distinction into a dualism of what a later idealism would call phenomenal and noumenal. It is not used in this absolute way by the writers of the New Testament, who speak of the resurrection as "spiritual" not to *exclude* the physical and material, nor to remove it from the phenomenal to the noumenal, but to point to the *transformation* of the material. If we are to speak rightly of Christ's resurrection, we must speak of an event which is "bodily", in that it concerns the material being of the Jesus who died, and yet "spiritual" in that it does not conform to the laws and normative patterns of material existence, but transforms the material in ways that require a different phenomenology and a different pattern of perception.

Cranmer then adds that Christ took "all things appertaining to the perfection of man's nature", that is to say, to a complete humanity (the Latin is *integritatem*), which made no concessions to a gnostic preference for the spiritual. It is not simply to be taken for granted that it was *human* nature which Christ brought back from death. Here, too, Cranmer casts a line back, relating the triumph of Easter to what has gone before it: to the incarnation, where he "took" human nature, and to the crucifixion where he bore its curse. The resurrection, too, then, is part of the history of that humanity, borne by our representative, whose vindication and perfection here is not for himself alone but on behalf of all men. To see the vindication of Christ as the vindication of his humanity is to see Easter as the climax to those other moments, which are more obviously moments of identification with humanity. There was one aspect of Good Friday, then, which Easter did not cancel: it did not cancel the representative "for us", but rather confirmed it, and brought it to its intended conclusion. "He was crucified for our sins, and raised for our justification" (Rom. 4:25).

And so we look back to what Article 2 tells us of Good Friday, in words taken more or less verbatim from the Augsburg Confession. Is there here a line thrown forwards? Does the Reformers' account of the cross expect Easter as its conclusion? It has often proved difficult for western theologies of the atonement to achieve this connexion convincingly. Anselm's mighty interpretation of the cross had little place for Easter, and Schleiermacher made what was in effect a confession of failure, on the part of the Anselmic tradition as well as his own romantic recasting of it, when he concluded that "it is impossible to see in what relation [the resurrection] can stand to the redeeming efficacy of Christ" (*Christian Faith* 99.1). Of Luther better things can be said, though it is not easy to draw out from him a systematic clarification of how the two events belong together. Neither is our short confessional statement clear on the matter; but it does offer an important hint.

It gives two reasons for Christ's death: "to reconcile his Father to us, and to be a sacrifice". That is, Christ's death accomplishes a movement in God and a movement in man. The movement in man is described as a "sacrifice". The full range of overtones which the concept of sacrifice carried in the Levitical law, and the wider range which it was later to acquire in romantic theology, were not known to the Reformers. We will read Cranmer and his mentors from Augsburg correctly if we understand the word to convey a simple Anselmic idea: the "sacrifice" of Christ is the reparation made to God's honour for the infinite offence of sin, the "sacrifice, oblation and satisfaction", as it is expanded in the eucharistic prayer, the "redemption [i.e., purchase price], propitiation and satisfaction" of Article 31. Man in Christ makes an offering, the only perfect offering that he can make.

The movement in God, on the other hand, is not an Anselmic idea. Here, too, Anselm and Schleiermacher (two interpreters of the atonement so often contrasted) are at one. Neither could easily accommodate the notion of a change in God's attitude, and it is for just that reason that neither can explain the connexion of the cross with Easter. For neither of them does the sequence of death and resurrection represent anything *in God*. Although the two interpret the cross very differently, they both see it as the perfect act of virtue by which the Redeemer accomplishes (or displays) the true relating of man with God. It is primarily a redemptive act, secondarily the matrix of our redeemed status (or consciousness). But in patristic thought the cross had been seen the other way round, primarily as a participation in the human plight, and secondarily (but only because it led to the resurrection) as a redemptive act. In the one case it is Christ's cross before it is ours, in the other it is ours before it is Christ's. But if Christ's death is (as the Fathers thought) an *identification* with man's plight, not (as Anselm maintained) simply a *prevention* of it, then we have conceived death in its relation to sin, as the expression of divine wrath. The negative judgment of God on man is no longer merely threatening, but actual (even though only emblematically) in the fact of common death; and the favourable judgment of God on men is an overcoming of wrath, just as the life and hope of man is an overcoming of death. When the Reformers speak of the "reconciling of [the] Father to us" they have in mind that the sequence of death and resurrection corresponds to a sequence in the judgment of God, and so they point us to the fulfilment of the cross in Easter.

If we speak in this way of the overcoming of divine wrath by divine favour, we will, of course, bear in mind what we said in the last chapter about sustaining the tension of paradox when speaking about God. We will speak of such a change in God only in the context of his unchangeableness, and we will speak of his wrath only in relation to the primacy of his love, the great Yes, pronounced on creation from the beginning, of which the No is merely the reverse side, the hostility of the Creator to all that would uncreate. We will speak of the wrath of God, as we speak of the suffering of God, dialectically; and we will not be too disturbed by objections which are themselves undialectical. Happily we are now rediscovering (is this not one undeniable strength of the theology of liberation?) that love which has no wrath on its underside is not love at all; that mankind cries out to see the sharp edge of justice and truth as surely as he cries out for love and compassion. Speech about the wrath of God is, in certain quarters, back in fashion. But such speech will lead us into a perilous fanaticism unless it extends to the *reconciliation* of divine wrath, and makes it the terminus of its thought, as it is the terminus of the biblical witness, to speak of God's favour. The God of the Psalms, "who is angry every day", has become favourable to mankind in Christ. He has not been banished, replaced by another and milder God — which would leave him and his anger dangerously unaccounted for, liable always to break out in rebellion at the behest of some religious passion. He has been reconciled, and therefore (from *this* point we can now say it) he has shown himself more truly and completely as the God who always *was* favourable to man in Christ, whose daily anger was never other than a zeal for the integrity of his beloved.

Here, then, is one way in which we are invited to see the two successive events, death and resurrection, linked, not arbitrarily as a mere reversal, but teleologically. The wrath of God gives way to his favour, in acknowledgement of the perfect sacrifice. This link should, in principle, be made clearer when we speak of the moment which stands between the two events, acting as a noetic connexion which interprets each in terms of the other: the descent to the dead. ("The dead" — for so we should translate the Latin *ad inferos*, avoiding the conventional English equivalent, "hell".)

As the Elizabethans left it to us, this Article simply affirms, in a manner designed to rebut docetic qualifications, the full reality of Christ's death. The Word of the Father was identified in every way with man's mortality, draining the cup to its dregs. And, as we have seen, such an affirmation is helpful, in that it qualifies the Anselmic inclination to treat the cross as a voluntary act of heroism, giving it the appearance of a new, pioneering achievement, rather than the suffering of an age-old fate. Yet Cranmer's original Article was, perhaps, even more helpful (though it raised more problems, to which we shall return shortly). It attempted to express the saving significance of Christ's death (*as* death, and not simply as heroism) by referring to the teaching of 1 Peter 3:19 (and 4:6) that the gospel was proclaimed to the dead. "The body lay in the sepulchre until the resurrection : but his ghost departing from him, was with the ghosts that were in prison, or in hell, and did preach to the same, as the place of S. Peter doth testify." The central meaning of the descent to the dead is that Christ's identification with mankind in death is at the same time a proclamation of God's favour, to those who are already dead, and so also to those who have still to die. The link between the cross and the resurrection is explicit. Already the conquest of death is preached. By making himself one with us in the darkness of God's wrath, Jesus brings us out from darkness into the light of God's favour. And in particular he brings those long dead: the place of St. Peter speaks of the generation who died in the primaeval flood, because they, alone among all generations, had no symbolic prefiguring of the Paschal Mystery to instruct them. They stand appropriately for all who have died without hearing the message of hope. To all who have lived and died in every age the one perfect work of identification and vindication extends its summons to rise from the grave and be alive for evermore.

This last point leads us naturally to consider how the Reformers understood the relation between the death of Christ and the incarnation.

The point about the crucifixion which the Reformers were anxious above all to maintain — and here we must include the whole

Reformation and not simply the English branch of it — was that this single happening was decisive for all history. "The offering of Christ once made is the perfect redemption, propitiation, and satisfaction for all the sins of the whole world," states Article 31. And in that sentence the most important phrase is "once made", echoing the repeated *hapax*, "once for all", of the Epistle to the Hebrews. As we are reminded by the situation of this statement — it occurs in Article 31 and not in Article 2 — the immediate occasion for the Reformers' contention was the controversy over the eucharist. But we would be short-sighted not to see behind the eucharistic controversy a much more important issue about the shape of history. The Reformers were striving to achieve a Christocentric idea of history. We see this not only in their battle against the concept of the Mass as repeated sacrifice, but also in their struggle for the authority of Scripture over tradition. That is why the legacy of the Reformation, though remote in many of its interests from ourselves, is of vital importance to us — for whom the battle between Kierkegaard and Hegel has shaped, and still shapes, our theological era.

In modern terms, what the Reformers defended was an eschatological conception of the work of Christ: that in his death and resurrection the end of the age was present; that his sacrifice is equally valid and equally immediate to every age, and not to be accounted for simply as the immanent product of one age and the inspiration of successive ones. To claim so much for Christ's death, of course, is implicitly to make the claim for his person. It raises the question of how we may so speak about Christ as to support the weight that is put upon these climactic events. We look, then, for a Christological statement which will suggest the eschatological character of Christ's appearing, a statement such as might have been modelled on the opening words of the Epistle to the Hebrews, the foundation for the "once for all" which echoes throughout that book: "In many and various ways God spoke of old to our fathers by the prophets; but in these last days he has spoken to us by a Son, whom he appointed the heir of all things."

We look in vain. The Augsburg Article which Cranmer followed took a conservative line, adopting the Anselmic principle that what was needed to sustain an understanding of the work of Christ was a Chalcedonian two-natures Christology: only man *should* make satisfaction, only God *could*. The Chalcedonian formula, then, introduces the clause on the atonement, and only the phrase "never to be divided" (*inseparabiliter coniunctae*) distantly evokes a sense of historical finality. Furthermore, the effect of interposing the two-natures formula *between* the main verb "took man's nature" and the clause "who truly suffered . . ." is to distance the first from the second.

The incarnation itself is no longer part of the story, but a preface to it, establishing the Christological conditions for the atonement. Contrast this with the sense of movement in Philippians 2:5ff., where the birth "in the likeness of men" is the first step in the twofold self-emptying of the one who was in God's form (controversially enough to many modern minds); or, again, with the Apostles' and Nicene Creeds. The coming of the Christ must *itself* unloose the climax of history; it is the breaking-in of the Kingdom of God, the coming of the Son of Man. It is true enough to say that only man should make satisfaction, only God could do so. But must we not say more than this, if we are to give the ringing affirmation of Article 31 its proper foundation? Must we not say that only the *new* man, the "last Adam", can represent all mankind in the offering of a new and acceptable sacrifice to God? And that only the coming of God's Kingdom can reconcile and recreate the world-order once given and now lost?

For the meaning of Christ's resurrection is that the renewal of all creation has begun. In a body that represents the "perfection" of man's nature we see the first-fruits of a renewed mankind and a sign of the end to that "futility" which characterizes all created nature in its "bondage to decay" (Rom. 8:19-21). There are two aspects to this renewal, which have to be kept in a proper balance. On the one hand we must not understand the newness of the new creation as though it implied a repudiation of the old. The old creation is brought back into a condition of newness; it recovers its lost integrity and splendour. In the resurrection appearances of Jesus the disciples were offered a glimpse of what Adam was always meant to be: lord of the elements, free from the horror of death. On the other hand, restoration is not an end in itself. Adam's "perfect" humanity was made for a goal beyond the mere task of being human; it was made for an intimacy of communion with God. The last Adam, in restoring human nature, leads it to the goal which before it could not reach, brings it into the presence of God's rule, where only the one who shared that rule could bring it. And so it is that the moment of triumph divides into two moments, a moment of recovery and a moment of advance. The resurrection must lead on to the ascension: "Do not hold me," said Jesus to Mary in the garden on the first Easter morning, "for I have not yet ascended to the Father" (Jn. 20:17). In the Western church we speak of God's deed as "salvation", emphasising the aspect of recovery and deliverance from sin and death. In the Eastern church they speak more commonly of *theosis* or "divinisation", emphasising the advance beyond simple restoration to communion with the divine nature. Both aspects are present; they are differentiated in the two steps of Christ's exaltation.

Differentiated, but not therefore torn apart. We cannot overlook the fact that of the four Gospels one, St. Mark, has nothing to say about the ascension; two, St. Matthew and St. John, hint at it allusively; and only one, St. Luke, narrates it as an event. In the theology of the Pauline epistles it remains, more often than not, undifferentiated from the resurrection. The ascension, we must judge, does not stand over against the resurrection as the resurrection stands over against the crucifixion; it does not add a new element to the story which was not present before, but unfolds the implications of what is present already in the resurrection. Are we, then, to agree with Barth's statement that "the empty tomb and the ascension are merely signs of the Easter event, just as the Virgin Birth is merely a sign of the nativity"?[1] No. For, as Barth himself elsewhere wished to say, what the ascension shows us of the meaning of Christ's triumph is *distinct*: it is the mark which defines *one side* of the resurrection, the elevation of Christ to the Father, and therefore stands in contrast to the landmark which defines the other side, the empty tomb. In between them, holding the two boundary-marks together into one triumphant happening, are the actual appearances of the risen Christ throughout the forty days.

This raises the question of how we are to understand the ascension as an *event*. Can the statement, "he ascended into heaven", stand alongside the statements, "he was crucified, died and was buried" and, "on the third day he rose again"? However problematic the statement of the resurrection may seem to be, the problems posed by the ascension are of a much more fundamental kind. For "heaven", "God's throne" and "the right hand of the Father" are not places that can be mapped topographically within space. The verb "ascended", like the verb "came down" in the creed, can refer to no form of spatial movement known to man.

The conventional modern metaphysic, which is a popularized version of Kant's, knows of only one other way to interpret these terms of place and movement, to which a phenomenal sense is so evidently inapplicable. It refers them to a realm of noumenal or mental reality. This idealist solution, which has proved popular among twentieth-century theologians, is the foundation for the suspicion, which has often been voiced against them, that they have in mind the conversion of Christian faith into a species of humanism. For whatever is not susceptible to location within our universe of space and time is assigned to Mind; but Mind turns out in the end either to be, or to be extremely like, the human mind, vested, for metaphysical purposes, in the robes of infinity. Classical Christianity knew of another possibility. Space and time are dimensions of our created universe; but God is not located within them, but beyond, as a craftsman is beyond the dimensions of what he has made. Modern

[1] *Church Dogmatics* III/2 tr. G.W. Bromiley et al., p. 453.

idealism itself, of course, posits a kind of "beyond"; but it posits it on the basis of that experience of transcendence which the human mind can know in thinking. The classical solution was not so ready to absolutise the experience of thinking. Even when it used it as an analogue, it understood that it must still point yet further "beyond", for the thinking mind, too, belonged in the here-and-now of creation. We shall not go wrong, then, in saying that the classical concept of transcendence was objective at points where the modern one is subjective.

Even in speaking of the transcendence of space and time I have used a spatial term, "beyond". In doing so I will not have been misunderstood; for when we use such terms in phrases of transcendence, "outside space and time", "before time began", or "above the highest heavens", our context indicates clearly enough that it is not a spatial "outside" or a temporal "before", but a metaphysical one. Yet in thinking of transcendence we are forced to use these spatial and temporal analogues, because we are ourselves spatial and temporal creatures and cannot think apart from the dimensions in which we live. Our imaginations are visual. Indeed, it is a famous problem of philosophy that we cannot even think of time itself without thinking of it spatially, as a line, a circle, a flowing stream or something such. If we have difficulty in thinking even of time, in which we exist and and which we experience immediately, without the aid of spatial images, it is not surprising that spatial images are necessary to help us think of what transcends space and time.

Christians believe that God, in the person of his Son, has established communication between his being and our created space-time order. How else can we speak of this communication except as "coming" and "going", as "up" and "down"? We say that Christ "came down from Heaven" and "ascended into Heaven", yet do not think of the incarnation and ascension as journeys through space from one location to another, like a journey between the earth and the moon. As Athanasius said wittily: "When Christ sat on the right hand of the Father, he did not put the Father on his left."[2] These events are transitions between the universe of space and time that God has made and his being which is (in a sense that we can apprehend, but not comprehend) beyond it. Yet these transitions are 'objective' in the sense that they cannot be reduced to states, or occurrences, of Mind. The incarnation is not simply a mythic portrayal of the fellowship between men and God, nor the ascension of the triumph of the cross. Insofar as these transitions have one foot in our space and time, they are seen there as *events* — events which, however, have another end

[2] *Contra Arianos* I.61.

to them beyond the historical sequence of which, at this end, they form a part.

With this in mind, let us think further about the ascension. Obviously, in one purely negative sense, it is an event in time: the resurrection appearances of Jesus came to an end. St. Luke makes it very clear that this is one important aspect of the ascension. It is the point at which Jesus is "taken from" the disciples until he is restored to them at the end of time (Acts 1:9, 11). Even St. Paul, who narrates his own vision of the risen Lord on the Damascus road as one of the resurrection appearances, acknowledges that it is "out of order" (1 Cor. 15:8). But there is more that must be said about the event than that it was the *cessation* of the resurrection appearances. It is not only a "taking from", it is a "taking up". It is a material event which involves the material body of Jesus; it leaves this spatio-temporal order to enter the immediate presence of the Creator. Article 4 is right to insert that important connective, "wherewith". This transition from the earth to Heaven is more than a reversal of the incarnation, at which God "came down"; it is the elevation of man, physical, spatio-temporal man, into an order that is greater than the physical and the spatio-temporal, and which is not his native habitat. What form does the human body take outside space and time as we know it? Obviously, that is the unanswerable question, the one which earns St. Paul's withering response, "You fool!". All we can say is that the transition has occurred, that there is a beaten path that lies before us, linking our physical existence to an existence in the presence of God which lies beyond its conditions. We cannot see the path — the cloud which hid Jesus on the mountain-top is a veil for that which cannot be comprehended from below — but we know that the path has been taken, and that we are to take it too.

In the same way that Jesus's ascension means the elevation of humanity beyond the limits of "our" space, it means also the elevation beyond the limits of "our" time. Here we must guard against the suggestion in Article 4 that Jesus is, as it were, killing time until his coming again: "he ascended . . . and there sitteth, until he return." There is nothing wrong with these verbs; they represent, quite properly, the different points at which Christ's triumph intersects with our time, past, present and future: he ascended, he sits, he shall return. But this time is *our* time; he is not bounded by it as we are, but is lord over it. We should not begin to ask what the ascended Lord is doing *in the meantime*, during the long wait before he must return. Traditional presentations of Christian doctrine have an item which they call the "Heavenly Session" of Christ, which speaks of what he is doing between the ascension and the parousia. Basing themselves on a verse in Hebrews (9:24), and another in Romans (8:34), they speak of

Christ's intercession before the presence of God for us, thinking of that intercession as a continual prayer of self-offering, a heavenly extension of the self-offering on the cross. When we read the relevant section of the Epistle to the Hebrews, however, we cannot help being struck by how the author sees the ascension as a decisive once-for-all act of intercession, not a long-drawn-out one. "He entered once for all into the Holy Place" (9:12). "Christ has entered . . . into heaven itself, now (i.e. at the moment of the ascension) to make his appearance before God's face for us" (9:24). "Nor was it to offer himself repeatedly . . . but he has appeared once for all at the end of the age" (9:25f.). Once the author speaks of a "waiting": "he sat down at the right hand of God, *then to wait* until his enemies should be made a stool for his feet" (R.S.V., 10:13). But even here the point of the verb "wait" — the "then" is a translators' elaboration — is not to bring out the *duration* of time, but the *expectancy*, that the subduing of his enemies should follow as the next thing.

What we see in the Epistle to the Hebrews is something very characteristic of the New Testament as a whole, the assertion that the Christ-event is the *last thing* in God's plan for the world, and that with its completion the end of time has, in effect, already come. We are seen to have our existence, as it were, in the middle of the end, in between the last things and the last things. Still to come is the universal manifestation of Christ's glory, but the time-lapse which separates that from the accomplishment of that glory in the ascension is of no significance. It serves the function of permitting the gospel to be preached to the end of the earth, but it does not add to, or subtract from, God's saving deed. Thus we find, both in the Scriptures and in the creeds, that the ascension and the parousia (the return) of Christ are seen together, almost as one event. When Christ sits down at the right hand of God, that is a gesture not of patient waiting but of triumph. The triumph is already achieved; it only remains for that triumph to be manifested universally. Christ ascended has reached the fulfilment of man's destiny; he is already at the end of time. Mankind will follow him to that fulfilment. Time is thus not an iron cage, within which all events are bound, but a dimension of history — and in the fulfilment of the purpose of history in Christ, we see that time, too, is fulfilled.

This will give us a new perspective, finally, from which we can think about the descent to the dead.

The descent to the dead is different, again, from the ascension, in that it has no point of intersection with our time-space universe. Dead bodies moulder and disintegrate in the earth where they are buried; they are not gathered together in one place. Jesus's body remained in its tomb in Jerusalem between his burial and his rising, and did not go anywhere in between. Cranmer, in affirming this, fell into difficulty because he admitted the point about space while still maintaining the appearance of an event within the same time-frame: "the body lay in the sepulchre until the resurrection : but his ghost departing from him, was with the ghosts that were in prison, or in hell." This interpretation had a long tradition, running back to the patristic period; but the difficulty with it was that it evoked a fundamentally mythical world of disembodied beings who are supposed to share our time but not our space. (Here, too, the failure to grasp the true sense of "in the spirit" at 1 Pet. 3:18 was fateful.) But just as the dead have no place within our space other than their tombs, so they have no existence at *this* point in our time except as memory or remains.

Yet that does not mean the dead do not have objective and real existence. There is a reality outside this created time-space order, and the dead are real because they are the object of God's judgement which confers reality upon them. That we cannot make their reality intersect with our bodily and temporal reality, that is the tragedy of death which we feel so deeply. But we know that the God who speaks to man of his moral responsibility passes judgement on the totality of a man's life when it is done. That judgement is the guarantee that the dead, too, are held in reality, though in a reality of a different order. We may have to think of this in temporal and spatial terms, as a *continuing* existence *somewhere* else — but this is the limitation of our thought. We do not believe literally either in a spatial "prison" for our spirits, or in a temporal "now" for their existence. They are held in being as the object of God's condemnation, as was Jesus when he entered into the full reality of human death. Yet now, ascended and glorified, he has his being in his unity with the Father and as the object of the Father's good pleasure. What "happened" in the descent to the dead is that they, who have their existence under the sign of judgement, were extended a new existence in the approval with which the Father views his Son. The confidence we now have about the believing dead is that they are united with Christ in his ascended glory. That extra-spatial "place" in which he is glorified, the Father's right hand, is their place also.

To us, of course, the ascended and glorified life is still future; it belongs to the end of time. And so we necessarily view the general resurrection of the dead as a *future* event, part of the public manifestation which we await. At the same time we think of Christ's descent to the dead as happening in the past, between the Friday afternoon and the Sunday morning, not because it took place then, but because it was *effected by* the crucifixion and the resurrection and stands between them noetically, making clear their relation to each other. We think, quite properly, that the liberation of the dead is something which *has been* accomplished. And we think of the blessedness of the dead as *present*. We remember Paul's conviction that to die was to gain more of Christ, and Jesus's promise to the thief on the cross, "Today you will be with me in Paradise," and we cannot believe that the dead are kept hanging around. The three tenses, the past present and future, are all points at which a reality beyond our time touches our time. They are all correct tenses to use. But we are mistaken if we try to systematize them into a series of temporal events which befall the dead, as though in our time, with hypotheses of intermediate states, purgatories and so on.

The Reformers were aware (who more so?) of the need to strip away the purely mythological beliefs which commonly comforted Christians in the face of death. In Article 22 we find that two of the five doctrines there singled out for condemnation concern death: the "Romish" doctrine of purgatory and the invocation of saints. If in Article 4 the purgation was not carried as far as it needed to go, that was not from lack of intent, but from the want of conceptual tools. A glance at two of the four eschatological Articles with which Cranmer's forty-two concluded, shows us how he proceeded, ruling out one after another unacceptable conception of death and resurrection until only one seems to be left. The resurrection is bodily and eschatological, not immanent and concerned only with the soul (39); the souls of the departed do not sleep until the day of judgement, nor do they die and rise again, together with their bodies (40). What does this leave to be said, other than that the soul abides with Christ until the day of bodily resurrection? But the conclusion, which the Articles themselves do not state but leave the reader to draw, depends upon the notions of a separable soul and of a single time-scale within which dead and living march in parallel through the years of waiting. Hence the mysterious "somewhere" of the dead, a spiritual enduring in a hidden realm, which is offered us as comfort as we lay our dead in that colder tomb than earth supplies, the grave of our oblivion. Yet such comfort is intrusive. Only upon those who have found no such consolation for their loss can the word of the gospel break, as it should break, with unhoped-for hope: Christ will bring the dead again with him at his appearing. If we would know Cranmer's mind on the matter, we must turn to the unforgettable opening sentences of his Burial Service, where the words of John 11:25f. express the Christian hope in terms utterly rooted in the achievement of Christ at the end of time: "I am the resurrection and the life, saith the Lord: he that believeth in me, yea though he were dead, yet shall he live. And whosoever liveth and believeth in me shall not die for ever."

3

THE SPIRIT AS AN AFTERTHOUGHT
(Articles 5)

The fourth Article followed the example of the creeds in taking the story of redemption directly from the ascension of Christ to his return. The creeds for their part, you might say, are simply following the two angels on the Mount of Olives, who said, "Men of Galilee, why do you stand looking into heaven? This Jesus, who is now taken from you into heaven, will come back in the same way that you have seen him go" (Acts 1:11). The angels had nothing to say about any intervening events between the departure and the return of Jesus. The whole content of the Acts of the Apostles was as though overlooked by them, as they directed the gaze of the church straight to the eschatological climax of history. I have already suggested some reasons why the ascension and the parousia should be held so closely together in this way.

But just as the disciples, having heard the angels' words, returned to Jerusalem and experienced there the wonder of Pentecost, the coming of "the promise of the Father", of which Jesus had spoken to them (Acts 1:4); so the creeds, having looked forward to the end, to the coming of Christ to judge the living and the dead and to the reign which shall have no end, return to the present, and begin the third article, "I believe in the Holy Spirit".

The reproduction of this order in the Articles is partly accidental, since we owe it to Parker, and not to Cranmer, that we have an Article on the Holy Spirit in this position. (In the Litany Cranmer did

differently, moving from the "glorious resurrection and ascension"
to the "coming of the Holy Ghost" and from there to "all time of our
tribulation, in all time of our wealth, in the hour of death, and in the
day of judgement.") But it is not to be brushed aside as a mere
curiosity. It teaches us how to think about the giving of the Spirit to
the church. We are not to think of it as an addition or supplement
to the work of Christ, as though that work was incomplete or half-
finished. If Pentecost were mentioned as the next thing after the
ascension, we might conclude that Christ's triumphant return to his
Father's glory was not the sign of an accomplished and finished work,
but only the penultimate or antepenultimate thing. Some Christians
have spoken in these terms, as though the whole work of Christ was
left hanging in the air and is constantly threatened with meaninglessness
unless the "next thing", which turns out to be human cooperation,
follows in quick order.

The gift of the Spirit at Pentecost is understood in the New
Testament not as a supplement to the ascension but as a fruit of it. The
triumph Christ has won is shared with mankind. "Exalted thus at
God's right hand, he received the Holy Spirit from the Father, as was
promised, and all that you now see and hear flows from him," said St.
Peter (Acts 2:33). St. Paul (in Ephesians 4:8) associates the "gifts of the
Spirit" (so-called elsewhere in his writings) directly with the ascended
triumph of Christ, quoting Psalm 68: "He ascended to the heights,
with captives in his train; he gave gifts to men." And since the
ascension is already, from God's point of view, the triumph of the
parousia and the Kingdom, so the experience of the Spirit, the fruit of
the ascension, is for us an anticipation of the coming Kingdom, a
"downpayment", as St. Paul twice describes it (2 Cor. 1:22; Eph.
1:14), of our inheritance.

But, it will be said with some justice, it is precisely the refusal to
allow that the Spirit contributes anything *additional* to Christ (and
this refusal, characteristic especially of Western theology, reaches its
height in the Reformation with its emphasis on the finished work) that
pushes the Third Person of the Trinity to the margin of Western
Christian thought. And here we must acknowledge that the omission
of an Article on the Spirit from the Edwardian Articles
(notwithstanding brief allusions in Articles on other subjects) was
indefensible. Whatever excuses may legitimately be made for Cranmer
on this point (e.g. that he was guided in his selection by polemical
concerns), there is no avoiding the impression — so properly alarming
to Eastern Christians — that the doctrine of the Spirit is reducible
without remainder to the doctrine of the Scriptures, the doctrine of
grace and the doctrine of the church.

Yet we may then add that this impression was apparently not

acceptable to the Tudor Anglicans as a whole — particularly, perhaps, those who had been exposed to the influence of Calvin's theology with its especially rich understanding of the Spirit — as the addition of Article 5 makes clear. What, then, is the *internal* necessity for a doctrine of the Spirit in Anglican theology? Why did it seem to the Reformers of the 1560's — as to us — that too little had been said?

An answer to this must follow two lines of thought. The first is that which we pointed to in the last chapter, the problem of the relation of the ascended Christ to our time, the time of the church and the believer. The ascension is an event in the past to us, and its full revelation is an event in the future. Our faith in the triumph of Christ focuses on what was, and on what will be. How, we must ask, can these events in the past and future be *present* realities to us? Or, to put it in a more satisfactory way, how can we move from our present time-reference to become contemporary to those events, past and future? How can we overcome the absence of Christ from our present? The Reformers were especially resistant to the suggestion that this question could be answered simply in terms of the continuity of the institutional church, and needed a further answer. A further answer was suggested in the farewell discourses of St. John's Gospel: "Now I am going to him who sent me, yet none of you asks me, 'Where are you going?' Because I have said this to you grief has filled your heart. But I tell you the truth, it is good for you that I go away. For if I do not go, the Advocate will not come to you; but if I go, I will send him to you" (John 16: 5-7). The Holy Spirit is the gift of God for the time of Christ's absence. He makes the reality of Christ's triumph present to us, and us to it; he connects the "there and then" with the "here and now".

The second line of thought is suggested by a passage in St. Paul's Epistle to the Ephesians, where Paul prays "that God may grant you to be strengthened with might by his Spirit in the inner man, that Christ may dwell in your heart by faith" (3:16f.). How does the reality of Christ, which is already a reality in the world, become inwardly present to us? How does that which God has wrought, and wrought completely, in Israel two thousand years ago touch the individual subjectively, to transform, not just the world in which he lives, but his inward being? The question was urgent to an age which had been fed on the subjective piety of the *devotio moderna* of the previous century. The answer, of course, must be that he believes in Jesus, and that this belief is a matter of personal commitment. But how does he believe? It is not enough to say, "God has done his part; now you must do yours." For him to believe in what God has done and to respond to it, itself requires a miracle of God. There can never be a point in my salvation at which God simply stops and leaves it to me.

The existential act of belief in Christ needs to be evoked in us by God himself. That is what the Holy Spirit does. He is God within me, prompting me to believe in God manifest in Christ, enabling me to approach God the Father. "In him we cry 'Abba, Father'. For the Spirit himself bears witness with our spirit, that we are God's children" (Rom. 8:15f.). Thus the Holy Spirit overcomes the problem of the objectivity and externality of God's saving deed in Christ. He makes the objective reality a subjective reality to us.

This train of thought was made explicit in one of the Edwardian Articles (Cranmer's tenth) which was omitted by the Elizabethans. Entitled "Of Grace", it began: "The grace of Christ, or the Holy Ghost by him given, doth take away the stony heart and giveth an heart of flesh." Parker missed something very important to the doctrine of grace when he failed to retain this connexion between divine grace and the Holy Spirit. As soon as we make this association, it is evident why we must be clear that the Spirit is nothing less than fully divine. He is, as Article 5 expresses it in the traditional Nicene terminology, "of one substance, majesty, and glory with the Father, and the Son, very and eternal God". The issue is whether we really have God dwelling within us. If we do not, what hope is there that we shall be able to respond in faith and obedience to the salvation wrought for us in Christ? At the same time, as soon as we make the association between the indwelling God and the Holy Spirit, we are delivered from the anxiety that divine grace may become some kind of usurpation of our agency. For the Holy Spirit is called the "paraclete" — the "advocate" or "counsellor" — one who stands beside us to help, not one who seizes the controls and runs our lives without consulting us. The phrase "the fellowship of the Holy Spirit" means what it says — that he keeps us company. The Anglican Reformers could have saved later generations a lot of problems if they had explicitly evoked the Holy Spirit in their doctrine of grace. In the next century we see the tendency for divine grace to be understood in terms of the providential direction of the world by the First Person of the Trinity, and to become increasingly deterministic, allowing no place for the free agency of man. We will have more to say about this when we discuss Article 17.

On the question of the *filioque* clause, no doubt, there is little hope that anything will be said that can offer a quick resolution to a longstanding and stubborn problem. In affirming that the Spirit proceeds "from the Father *and* the Son" the Article echoes that interpolated version of the Nicaeno-Constantinopolitan creed which was universal in the West by the late middle ages. The meaning and appropriateness of this additional clause is, perhaps, the most vexatious of the problems which divide Eastern Christians from Anglicans today.

As with most ecumenical stumbling-blocks which arise from long tradition, it would be inadvisable to think that we could take a short way with the *filioque*. Although its presence in Tudor formularies was, no doubt, a matter of course, it is not the case that Anglicans have never thought or cared about it: the theologians of the seventeenth century did attend to the problems it created, and did defend it. Furthermore, at the time of the Reformation itself, the memory was not so very distant of the last major effort to persuade the East to accept the Western formula at the Council of Florence in 1439. That the very discussion strikes strangely on the ears of many contemporary Anglicans is not sufficient reason to conclude that it can be abandoned without thought — a gesture which would hardly please those Eastern Christians who regard it as eminently worthy of the most careful thought. Nevertheless, there is one step that can be taken quickly. Acknowledging that it has no place in the original text, we can omit it when we say the creed (as the Moscow Agreed Statement of Anglican-Orthodox Dialogue recommended in 1977). This does not imply its omission from other liturgical formularies (such as the Litany) or from hymns (such as the *Veni Creator*), nor any concession on the ground of its doctrinal appropriateness. Some Anglican churches have ordered this omission already. It is high time the others did so.

As for the substance of the *filioque*, there is a crucial point on which Orthodox and Anglicans agree. The gift of Pentecost was the gift of the ascended Christ. This is of very great importance; it means that the presence of the Spirit in the Church does not in any way go *beyond* the triumph of Christ. From time to time there have arisen movements of revival in the church which, in their enthusiasm to stress the reality of God's presence in our midst, have succumbed to a temptation to rejoice in the revelations, prophecies, miracles and powers which the Holy Spirit manifests in the church, but not to rejoice, or not very much to rejoice, in the witness which he bears to Jesus of Nazareth as the exalted Son of God. The Montanists of the second and third centuries used to say that with the coming of the Spirit history had entered a new age, the age of the Spirit, which went beyond the age of the Son and brought a superior revelation. (Such speculations about history also marked the highly influential thought of Joachim of Fiore in the twelfth century.) New truth was now made known to the church, which had not been made known by Jesus; new powers were given to the church which Jesus had not given; the gift of Pentecost went beyond the gift of Christmas, Easter and Ascension. Here we see again the significance of the order in which the creed and the Articles treat of the Spirit: Pentecost is not *added* to the sequence, Christmas, Easter, Ascension, as a further and additional moment of divine revelation, but rather stands apart from them, casting light back on them and interpreting them. The Spirit "who proceeds from the Father", says Jesus in the farewell discourse of St. John's Gospel, is also the Comforter "whom I will send you from the Father" and he "will bear witness of me" (Jn. 15:26). "He will glorify me, because he will take what is mine and make it known to you" (Jn. 16:14).

On this, as I say, there is no disagreement between Orthodox and Western Christians. When Eastern Christians deny the appropriateness of saying that the Spirit proceeds from the Son, they do not mean to deny that at Pentecost he was sent from the Son upon the church. They mean, rather, to mark a distinction between the coming of the Spirit in salvation history and the relations between the three persons of the Trinity in the being of the godhead, between the "temporal" and "eternal" processions of the Spirit. It is in *that* context that they shrink from saying that the Spirit owes his being to the Father *and* the Son, rather than to the Father alone. And here, too, the Western Christian can show some sympathy. For theologians in the West (and not least Augustine, who first articulated the double procession of the Spirit) have also constantly said that the Father is the sole "fount of godhead"; and that this distinguishes his *persona* from that of the Son and the Spirit. And Western Christians can admit that some of the language that has been used in the West of the eternal procession has been, at the least, misleading, and has tended to obscure this common confession of the unique primacy of the Father. (It has been unhelpful, for example, to speak of the Father and the Son as "cause" of the Spirit's being; and the observation of Augstine that they constituted "one origin" could be, and has been, misunderstood to suggest that the Spirit originated in the abstract divine essence common to Father and Son, and not (as intended) in their interaction as *personae*.)

But the Western theologian cannot happily accept the principle that there are things to be said about the persons of the godhead in their eternal relations which are *different* from what we say about their action in salvation-history. How could we know anything about the being of God other than what God himself has shown us in making himself known in Jesus Christ? How could we ever say: "God in Christ looks like this, but God-in-himself looks like that?" There is a crucial issue of epistemology here which prevents us following the Eastern theologian into what looks like irresponsibly abstract speculation.

However, that is not all that can be said on the matter. For in the very revelation of God in Jesus (and not in some speculative region which is supposed to lie behind it) we see not one but two ways in which the Spirit relates to the Father and the Son. The Spirit is acknowledged in the New Testament before Pentecost, and in a distinctively trinitarian context. At the baptism of Jesus by the Jordan, St. Mark tells us, as Jesus "came up out of the water, he saw the havens opened and the Spirit like a dove descending upon him; and there was a voice from heaven, 'You are my Son, the beloved; in you I am well pleased' " (Mk. 1:10f.). Here the three persons of the Trinity are revealed in the relation that is proper to them: the Father, declaring his good pleasure in his Son; the Son, the object of his good pleasure; and between them the Spirit, proceeding from the Father as a witness that the Father loves and owns the Son. If we take this moment, rather than the moment of Pentecost, as our guide, then we are certainly not departing from God's self-revelation; we are, in fact, standing at the very centre of it, at the Christological relation itself, in order to understand not only the Son's relation to the Father and the Father's to the Son, but the relation of each to the Spirit. St. Basil saw the importance of this starting point when he interpreted the place of the Spirit in the Trinity in terms of the Father's anointing of the Son: the Son as the anointed one, the Father the one who anoints, and the Spirit the anointing.[1] Indeed, Pentecost, we might claim, is the *wrong* starting point, because the Spirit is there concerned inescapably with the formation of the church; and we must therefore presuppose a prior moment, a relation of the Spirit to the Father and the Son in which the believing church is not yet present, except implicitly in the person of the Son.

Here, it would seem, is a point of departure which may afford a real opportunity for the convergence of the two traditions, and which (more importantly than that) may simply be the right way to think about the tri-personal godhead. It satisfies the Orthodox desire to get "behind" Pentecost to inter-trinitarian relations, but without pretending to get behind the revelation of God in Christ. Furthermore, it shows up both what is legitimate and what is illegitimate in the understanding of the double procession.

On the one hand, it was a model something more like this that was in Augustine's mind when he first spoke of procession from the Father and the Son. It was not the Pentecostal pattern that concerned him, in which the Father and the Son jointly sent the Spirit upon the church; it was the Father's love for the Son which, in his theological exploration, provided the initial model for the Trinity. And although Augustine's conception of the eternal bond of love is not precisely the same as the picture offered us in the synoptic gospels, the pattern is compatible enough. In such a pattern the priority of the *Father* is clearly maintained; yet the point of importance to Augustine and the West is also safeguarded: that it is not a matter simply of the Father leading forth the Spirit out of himself, but that it is in the Father's relation to the *Son* that the Spirit has his source of being — from the Father! This

[1] *De Spiritu Sancto* 12.28

is the true meaning of the contentious *unum principium*: that the love *of* the Father *for* the Son is the *one* occasion for the Spirit's hypostatic being — it is not a question of cooperation or collusion. There must be, in any statement of this kind, a disequilibrium between Father and Son, a unidirectionality which places the Father as subject and the Son as object of the divine love — and theologians of the *filioque* have often failed to do justice to this disequilibrium in their concern to maintain the reciprocity of the love between the Father and the Son. At the same time it must be in the relation of the Father *to the Son* that the Spirit's being is established and not in the Father alone, with Son brought in as an afterthought — and this, it would appear, is what the various Orthodox attempts to approach the Western position (such as by speaking of the 'manifestation' of the Spirit from the Son) have so far failed to achieve.

4

THE SCRIPTURES
(Articles 6—8)

In the first five Articles the English Reformers rehearsed in traditional terms their faith in God as Trinity, in the incarnation, crucifixion, resurrection, and Holy Spirit, as they had received it from the early centuries of the church's development and as they held it in common with their theological adversaries, at least those on the Roman side. There was little polemical material in those articles, and what there was was directed, more incidentally than deliberately, at Unitarian trends that emerged on the radical wing of the Reformation.

In the sixth, seventh and eighth articles everything has changed. Here we encounter the epistemological principle that was, more than anything else, more, even, than the doctrine of justification by faith, the hallmark of the Reformation at large: the authority and sufficiency of Holy Scripture. Not everything that the document has to say about Scripture is included in these three articles: the subject recurs in Article 20, where it is said that the Church may not so expound one place of Scripture that it is repugnant to another, and again in Article 21, where it is said that the decrees of General Councils touching matters necessary to salvation have neither strength nor authority unless they can be shown to be derived from Scripture. It is worth pondering on what this division of the subject matter implies.

We have, in the first place, Scripture, a collection of books which may be listed by their titles, thirty-eight of them in the Old Testament and a further twenty-seven, which are so uncontroversial that they need no listing, in the New; and the task is to define the limits of

Scripture and explain the authority which it possesses. In the second place, we have the exposition of Scripture, the corporate interpretation of the sacred text which constitutes the evangelical heartbeat of the church's life, and some limited directions as to the way in which this exposition may proceed. We must be struck at once by how different this organization of things is from what has become almost unquestionable in modern discussions. It is not so much that the exposition of the Scripture is thought of as an activity of the *church* (which is familiar enough to us) — but that it is thought possible to treat of Scripture and its authority quite separately from the question of how it is interpreted. What we would nowadays call "hermeneutics" is considered as a distinct question, which follows from other questions, already asked and answered, about the limits of Scripture and its authority. This approach is strikingly characteristic of the Anglican reformation. It reminds us that one of the earliest acts of the Henrician reform was the placing of an English Bible in churches; and that Cranmer's famous preface to the 1549 Prayer Book was principally concerned with defending the reform of the lectionary and Psalter — the ordered *reading* of Holy Scripture, rather than the *exposition* of it, being the centre of Anglican worship. Scripture is independent of, and prior to, the church's exposition of Scripture, and the church relates to it, in the first place, simply by reading it aloud and only secondly by preaching. The implication is clear: the books of Scripture are not authoritative because the church views them in a certain way; the church views them in a certain way because they are authoritative.

Nevertheless, it is still the case that the statements about Holy Scripture in Articles 6-8 are conceived as a theological *epistemology*. That is to say, they tell us about the order of knowledge, not about the order of reality. If this were not what was intended, then the assertion "Holy Scripture containeth all things necessary to salvation" would be blasphemous. In the order of reality, it is Jesus who contains all things necessary to salvation, who is the locus of God's self-giving and self-revelation. God was incarnate in a man, not a book. Complaints about the "bibliolatry" of modern conservative Christians often focus on this point — and in principle they are right to do so. Even if such complaints have not always been made in good faith, with the serious intention of being responsible to the revelation of God, who would dare say that they have never been justified? The Articles, at least, are not inclined to bibliolatry, as is clear enough from their whole mode of proceeding as well as from the statement of Article 7: "Both in the Old and New Testament everlasting life is offered to mankind by Christ, who is the only mediator between God and man."

The puzzle for the modern reader is to conceive of how there may be a way of knowledge (which does not overstep its bounds and lay claim to become the thing known) that is not defined entirely in terms of the knowing subject. How can we speak of the way in which God's self-disclosure is known, without (as we say) "beginning where we are", with our modern exercise of reading the Scriptures and trying to make something of them from our modern point of view? How can there be any knowing that is not knowing *by us*? — and by "us" we usually mean an abstractly conceived, modern man, sceptically disposed to almost everything, though we may sometimes mean (equally abstractly) a jolly modern Christian layperson, participating freely in coffee and biscuits at a Bible-study group. Our difficulty is entirely created by a one-sided conception of knowledge in general. We fail to see that the way of knowing any given thing is dictated in large measure by *what that thing is*, and not only (or even mainly) by the situation of the person who has come to know it. This is why pre-modern Christianity had no difficulty saying, what strikes us as so strange, that there is a *way of access* to the knowledge of God's saving deeds in Christ, which is presupposed by our actual access, an authoritative sphere wherein Christ is made known, which commands the way in which he actually becomes known *to us*. And that authoritative sphere is Scripture.

This is not an arbitrary decision. Scripture is authoritative precisely because of what it is and contains: within it "everlasting life is offered to men by Christ". It testifies in a decisive way to the historical event of the incarnation. Only on that ground can any book belong to the canon and count as Holy Scripture. The early patristic church, in its debate about the definition of the New Testament canon, laid the very greatest weight on apostolicity — not, that is, on apostolic authorship narrowly conceived, but on general apostolic provenance. It expected to be reasonably satisfied that a book which laid claim to canonical status was of an apostolic date and arose from some circle with close access to apostolic teaching. The authority of the New Testament is essentially the authority of the apostolic circle. And the apostles have authority on two counts: because they were eye-witnesses of what God did among men in Jesus, and especially of his resurrection, and because they were commissioned by Jesus to bear his message, and the message about him, to the world. In the final analysis, then, the New Testament has no authority which is not the authority of Jesus and the authority of the mighty acts of God involving him. But, correspondingly, the authority of Jesus and of these events is (from an epistemological point of view) vested entirely in the New Testament, and communicated exclusively through its witness. There is no other route by which those events make themselves known to later generations.

The positive statement, "Holy Scripture containeth all things necessary", implies, therefore, a position hostile to the claim for an unwritten apostolic tradition, handed down orally through the early church and providing an independent and complementary access to the apostolic faith and practice. The Council of Trent had resurrected this centuries-old claim at its fourth session in 1546; and although the Articles make no explicit reference to it, it forms the background to their discussion of Scripture and tradition. The statement of Article 6, we say, rules out the idea of an unwritten apostolic tradition, although it is obviously possible to conceive of a non-scriptural tradition that did in fact go back to the apostles and was yet not "necessary to salvation". (An example might be the association of St. Peter with the see of Rome.) But such a tradition, however apostolic from a purely historical point of view, could not be regarded as carrying *apostolic authority*; it was not part of the apostolic witness to the facts and meaning of what God had done in Christ. The problem lies in the appeal to such a tradition as the authoritative grounds for Christian life and practice. But could it not, we might wonder, have authority without actually being "necessary to salvation"? Could we not think that true Christian faith must indeed recognize the claim of the Roman see to exercise the authority of Peter, while yet allowing that those who denied or doubted would not suffer the fires of hell? Such a train of thought would put a construction on the words "necessary to salvation" which is hardly to be credited to the Reformers' intentions. They were not in the business of defining a *minimum* content of Christian faith which, however deficient, would suffice to ensure the believer his place in the Kingdom of Heaven — and nor should any of us be in that doubtful business. "Necessary to salvation" can mean one thing only: that it is pertinent to the gospel of Jesus Christ, which demands of us, for the salvation of our souls, our total faith and obedience. Belief in Christ is indivisible. None of us can say of another person's defective faith whether God will recognize it as faith in Christ or not; we can only say of ourselves that if we refuse obedience to what we see to be intrinsic to the gospel, then we are, by implication, refusing Christ. This principle will become explicit in another context, in Article 14.

Laying claim to an unwritten tradition is one of two ways in which the church may assert its own authority against the authority of the apostolic witness in the New Testament. The other way (which is also the more modern way, since belief in the existence of an unwritten apostolic tradition has fallen out of favour on scholarly grounds) is to maintain the accrual of authority to longstanding beliefs and practices, to the point where they become treated as premises in every argument, never as conclusions, and so stand on an equal footing with the teachings of Scripture. I say, the church asserts its *own* authority; for it is important to see that in speaking of the authority of tradition we are not speaking of the authority of past practices but of the present ones. Nothing is "tradition" unless it is believed or practised *today*. Though it certainly has the sanction of custom, the essential thing about "tradition" is the "handing on", and when handing-on stops, the tradition is no longer a tradition but only a memory. Tradition, then, is the life and faith of the contemporary church, insofar as it is in continuity with that of immediately preceding generations; its authority is the authority of continuity with the nearer past, the authority to go on doing and thinking what this generation has been brought up to do and think. The question is: what authority do we have to do that? What are the proper claims of conservatism?

For clarity we ought to distinguish two different aspects of the question; on the one hand the question of non-scriptural *formulations of faith* — for example, the term *homoousios* in the Nicene creed — and on the other the question of non-scriptural *ecclesiastical institutions* — for example, monarchical episcopacy. The Articles treat of the two separately, dealing here with the question of tradition in dogma, and in later Articles (especially 34) with institutions. We may say as a generalization that they are more generous to traditional institutions than to traditional dogmas; yet we should notice that there is a consistent approach to the two aspects of the question, which may be summed up in three ways: (a) they incline to favour traditions common to the universal church and of patristic antiquity; (b) they assert the freedom of the church with respect to tradition, over against the obligation of the church with respect to Scripture; (c) they qualify the church's freedom only as far as is necessary to safeguard the freedom of the individual believer not to have improper burdens imposed on his conscience, faith or vocation. This constitutes an approach which is, and has remained, distinctively Anglican, unlike the Roman approach on the one hand, with its higher valuation of tradition, and unlike other Protestant approaches, which tend to pay less respect to patristic traditions, and have often laid greater stress on the freedom of the individual believer.

In Article 8 the English Reformers take their stand in relation to dogmatic tradition in the form of the three creeds traditionally accepted in the mediaeval Western church as embodying the faith of the universal church of the patristic era: the Apostles', Nicene, and Athanasian creeds. As is customary, we murmur a word of regret that they chose these three documents to sum up the patristic legacy, the Apostles' Creed weighed down as it is with mediaeval developments, and the Athanasian creed being not, in truth, a creed at all, but only an individual composition and of Western provenance at that. The misjudgement of sixteenth-century theologians on such matters (which seventeenth-century researches would disclose) is a happy illustration of the very problem which impelled the church towards a scriptural reformation in the first place: the capacity of doubtful dogmatic traditions to cover themselves with borrowed pretensions. Nevertheless, it is clear what the Reformers wished to establish by their selection of documents: points of contact with the pre-Nicene church, with the Niceno-Constantinopolitan settlement of the trinitarian question, and with the Chalcedonian settlement of the Christological question (to which the Athanasian creed gave the most convenient documentary access). And in establishing these contacts with the church of the first five centuries they intend to be free of the opinions of any individual theologian, however great, and associate themselves only with the most considered doctrinal confessions of the church speaking as a whole.

There were, of course, many voices to be heard in the sixteenth century (as today) which would have counselled the Anglican Reformers to dispense with the doubtful blessing of a dogmatic tradition expressed in terms unknown to Christ and his apostles. It is much to their credit that they refused such advice. They realized, as Athanasius in his day had realized, that to restrict theology to the actual words of Scripture was to inhibit its critical task. Any form of words, even the scriptural ones, can be pressed to accommodate opinions hostile to their original intent. Words are a soft material, their sense easily eroded by the weathering of time, through genuine misunderstanding or through dialectical cleverness. The task of biblical exegesis is to restore and maintain the clear outline of the scriptural sense, assisting the reader to hear the words of Scripture with the force which they had at their first uttering, so that they are effective in bringing to critical examination the ideas and speculations which prevail at any given age. But exegesis is not simply reading over the text, though its aim is to facilitate reading. It uses other words; it must do so if the words before it are to be "drawn out" (as the term "exegesis" suggests) to reveal their sense. To refuse theology the use of other words is to refuse exegesis; and to refuse exegesis is to refuse the critical impact of the Scriptures, and to protect one's ideas and speculations, which can perhaps make peace with the *words* of Scripture, from any serious criticism or examination before the *sense* of Scripture.

The dogmatic tradition, therefore, offers us a paradigm of the task of theology, and its achievements are to be taken seriously. The patristic dogmatic tradition had the additional advantage, in the Reformers' eyes, of pre-dating the first major divisions of the church and the arrogation of a false authority to the Roman See, which (with a somewhat one-sided perception) they understood as a major influence in the corruption of biblical truth. They attached themselves to the patristic tradition at those points where its achievements were most thoroughly thought through — the Trinitarian and Christological dogmas — and they did so not unaware that there was much in the thought and practice of the patristic era which anticipated later false directions or was in itself purely bizarre. The somewhat puzzled affection and respect for the patristic era, so characteristic of successive generations of Anglican theology, was present at the beginning. But there was no formal reason given for it. The only principle they mention in relation to the patristic creeds is something that could be said of any theology of any age which was valued by succeeding ages: they are to be "believed, for they may be proved by most certain warrants of Holy Scripture". The value of the fathers' contribution to our theology has always to be measured against Scripture itself. It never goes without saying that what they achieved and defined was right; it is our duty to satisfy ourselves of that by measuring their work against the apostolic witness.

"The most certain warrants of Holy Scripture" are not, of course, proof-texts for the concepts and terms with which the fathers expressed their faith. There could be no such proof-texts. Since those concepts and terms are intended precisely to *draw-out* the force of the scriptural words, it is obvious that the scriptural words themselves (*qua* words) cannot validate them. If the author of a catechetical handbook writes, "Christ died for the sins of the whole world" and then adds the reference, "1 Jn. 2:2", he is validating his claim by drawing attention to an actual verbal echo. If an exegete writes: "The term 'world' refers to the human community as a whole, understood as being in rebellion against God," or if a dogmatician refers to the "universality" of salvation in Christ, there will (simply by virtue of the different nature of the task) be no such reference — or if there is, it will serve a different function. Yet in these cases, no less than in the first case, the adequacy of what the theologians have said will be measured by the Scriptures. If we would judge of this adequacy, we must read through the Scriptures with them, pose the questions they posed in the light of them, weigh the answers they gave. And if we find their work good, we may confidently adopt their conclusions and their concept-ualisations, making them our own, yet all the time knowing that they are still answerable to scripture. The map may be excellent — possibly even faultless. Yet precisely because it *is* a map, it is answerable to the countryside, not the countryside to it. The experienced walker does not assume too quickly that the map is in error; yet the question of its adequacy can never be settled absolutely, once and for all. And so it is with our guides in theological exploration. They are our seniors, much to be respected and never to be scorned; we will always, if we are wise, assume that we have much to learn from them. Yet we learn from them best when we hear them critically, testing and proving the value of their work against the measure which judges all theologians equally and without respect of persons.

But to our modern perceptions, shaped by traditions of questioning so different from those of the sixteenth century, all that we have said so far must ᵣᵒem out of place, like a manoeuvre of procrastination, staged to delay our encounter with the central and most difficult question which a scriptural theology must meet: how can we continue to treat the Bible as an authority, when we read it not as a unity but as a diversity? So pressing is this question to Christians of our own age (whether "conservative" or "liberal" — for those labels do not indicate any profound disagreements about the agenda for discussion) that it is a healthy exercise of thought to endure a little procrastination over it. It is better to wait upon the priorities of another age than to rush in with loud insistence upon our own. But we cannot follow the order of the Articles any further than this, but must bring forward the thesis which the Tudor authors were happy to defer until Article 20: that the church may not "so expound one place of Scripture, that it be repugnant to another".

The very presence of such a thesis show us that they were not altogether unconscious of the pressures which have led us to put all the weight of scriptural authority onto the question of "hermeneutics". They had had sufficient experience of diversifying expositions of Scripture to know that they had negative implications for the question of authority. They knew that it was not enough to assert the authority of the sacred text and simply leave the hermeneutical question wide open. They had met polemical arguments which accommodated comfortably enough the *formal* claim for Scripture, but which made such great play with the diversities and contradictions as to rob that formal claim of all its substance. The ordinary reader, it was suggested, could only be bewildered by the biblical text, and so, for all practical purposes, must resign himself to the teaching authority of the church. In response to such disingenuous arguments, the Reformers were prepared to insist, if not on the good sense of the ordinary reader of Scripture, at least upon the *ordinary readability* of Scripture, without which the attribution of authority to Scripture would be a mere *pro forma* gesture. Yet if Scripture is ordinarily readable, there must be a unity and coherence to it. The readability of the whole is not established merely from the readability of its various constituent books and texts. Unless we can think that Scripture is readable as a whole, that it communicates a unified outlook and perspective, we cannot attribute doctrinal authority to it, but only to some part of it at the cost of some other part. The authority of Scripture, then, presupposes the possibility of a harmonious reading; correspondingly, a church which presumes to offer an unharmonious or diversifying reading may be supposed to have in mind an indirect challenge to the authority of Scripture itself.

This is what the Reformers thought; and in expressing that thought they appropriately placed their prohibition of diversifying interpretations under the heading of the church's teaching authority. The difference in our position today is that we cannot make this last supposition with them. We cannot impute a sceptical intention to every diversifying interpretation of Scripture. This may seem a strange observation to make at the end of an era which has demonstrated beyond question that the prevalence of diversifying interpretations does, indeed, breed scepticism on a large scale, an era marked by a painful loss of confidence in scriptural authority and by a petulant wilfulness in theological utterance at every level, from the most scholarly to the most popular. Yet it is the case. The hold which diversifying interpretations have gained upon the mind of the church over the past century and a half is attributable, not simply to the perennial cry of "Let us break their bonds asunder", but to a positive discovery: that reading for contrast, rather than simply reading for harmony, can be wonderfully illuminating of the text. At the heart of the modern difficulty with the authority of Scripture is the simple fact that there is a modern tradition of reading the Scriptures, which genuinely is a tradition of *reading* and not of destructive dialectic, yet which is itself dialectical to the extent that it depends upon doing precisely what Article 20 instructs us not to do.

The sixteenth century could hardly have imagined such a thing to be possible. Indeed, even for us it is easier to say that it *is* the case than to say *how* it is the case; for reading must be directed to discerning a unifying sense within a text, which is to say, to treating it as *one* text; and a policy of dismemberment must appear *prima facie* to be a policy of *not* reading. Yet our experience is that within the modern tradition, too, we have been helped to read the Bible — not necessarily better than our forefathers read it, but differently, so that we have become responsible for what our own kind of reading has discovered there. And that means that we cannot simply repent of the modern tradition of reading and put it behind us, as would be appropriate with a sin or a temptation; for that would be to turn our backs on the Bible, a refusal no less serious than the scepticism to which the modern tradition itself can tempt us. The intellectual task which has faced the church ever since the modern tradition came to prevail within it is to

58 On the Thirty Nine Articles

appropriate it critically. Among the faithful it has always been controversial (one of its many ill effects has been the gulf between the body of not uneducated church members and a self-conscious élite of biblical scholars), and among practitioners of other neighbouring intellectual disciplines its excesses have always made it suspect. Today there are more signs than before that its weaknesses are understood within the theological community itself — perhaps because its powers of illumination are nearly spent — and there is some possibility of a critical reappraisal of what it has given us, and why its gift has left us in dreadful disarray.

What is this "modern tradition of reading"? I have chosen the phrase in order to avoid the title customary among scholars, "critical method", a highly misleading expression. It suggests that the heart of the modern tradition is methodological: that is, that it applies certain abstractly-formulated systems of enquiry, perfected independently and in other contexts, to the material of Scripture. Although it is true that this is what many scholarly practitioners set out to do, it is doubtful whether they actually do it, and more or less certain that none of the really important contributions made to our understanding of the Bible in the modern period has been achieved in this way. On the contrary, it is the methodological self-consciousness of the modern biblical scholar, his determination to impose a pre-planned programme of interpretation irrespective of the violence it may do to the text, which has produced that incessant flow of exaggerated absurdities which scornful observers unkindly call his "assured results". When we add the epithet "critical" to the term "method", the obscurity becomes worse. We imagine that there is one critical method, a kind of universal system of enquiry which will serve its turn on any material, whereas in fact the history of modern scholarship is that of constantly replacing one method with another. The origin of this term was, of course, the nineteenth-century application to scriptural study of the so-called "higher criticism" — a phrase which acknowledges that there is, in fact, more than one form of critical investigation and refers quite particularly to *historical* enquiry, undertaken with the then current Hegelian view that every concept is attained and comprehended only through a dialectical history of ideas.

To explain why the modern tradition of reading has been successful (and its success does need explaining, given the doubtfulness of so many of its scholarly conclusions) is to explain why historical enquiry — and particularly that motivated by Hegelian conceptions of history — could be illuminating when applied to the Bible. And that, surely, must be because a belief in sacred history is one of the fundamental elements in Christian faith itself. And the Hegelian conception of history is peculiarly suited to illuminating the Bible, precisely because the concept of history which Hegel applies, with only intermittent success, to universal history is so evidently a concept of *sacred* history, and therefore not only suitable to, but implicitly derived from, the reading of the Scriptures. We may notice, as a matter of curiosity, that modern biblical studies have had two major points of fruitfulness, and in both of them they have been under strong philosophical influence: one in the nineteenth century under the tutelage of Hegel and one in the twentieth century under the tutelage of Kierkegaard. But the great argument between Kierkegaard and Hegel was always an implicitly theological one, over how history is to be understood and over how the eternal interacts with the historical in the Christian understanding of revelation. So far from disapproving of the philosophical influences on biblical study as a non-scientific distortion, we ought rather to think that it is just these influences which have given the modern tradition of biblical study its authenticity as a theological enterprise, so that it has offered (with whatever excesses) a reading of Scripture that responds to issues which Scripture itself raises, and which must dominate any scripturally oriented thought.

If we wish to understand what it means to say that Jesus is "the Christ", we must come to grips with the history of the Messianic idea in the Old Testament. That is the way in which the Holy Spirit has expounded the concept of the Christ for us. But the history of the idea in the Old Testament is a history of change and transformation. It is not simply a matter of seeing a "type" of the Messiah in the Davidic king. We have to comprehend the history of kingship itself, including its rejection by God in the Babylonian captivity (with the consequent vacuum of political authority and theocratic authenticity) which is the negative side of the proclamation of the Kingdom of God, preparing the way for the emergence of the transcendent Son of Man from the anointed king, the "Son of God". We have to comprehend the ambivalence in Israel about the origins of the monarchy, the tussle between the theocratic and the monarchic ideals, in order to see how the Messianic expectation which emerges brings together the notions of mediate and immediate divine rule. But in order to trace this history, we must be able to distinguish the successive voices that emerge at us from the Old Testament: distinguishing them historically, so that we can tell the voice of Messianic monarchism in the royal psalms from the voice of transcendent post-monarchical Messianic expectation; and also distinguish them thematically, so that we can tell the voice of anti-monarchic theocratic prophetism from that of monarchist legitimism in the early period. So we are caught up, then, in pointing contrasts between one moment in the story and another, in a diversifying pattern of interpretation which seizes upon the ways in which one part of the Scripture sounds differently from another. We do it, not because we are refusing to treat the Bible as the Bible, but because this is the actual character of the Bible (or rather of the Old Testament) that we have before us: it is the record of an emerging theological idea, concretised and lived out in a society whose history is woven together with that of the idea.

Is this, in effect, to debunk the Christological concept, to rob it of its meaning by showing it up as the product of centuries of chance evolution and sociological conflict? On our answer to this will depend our attitude, not simply to the modern tradition, but to the biblical revelation itself. For we cannot avoid the conclusion that this is, in effect, how the Scriptures show us God making himself known. What if we say that God *cannot* be made known in this way — that this is not a way in which anything of eternal significance *may* be known? Then we are simply rejecting the biblical God, who makes himself known by acts in history, whose self-revelation, therefore, must take the form of history. This is not to embrace modern historicism, with its denial of eternal truths and its opposition to metaphysics. It is merely to say that (within the Scriptures, at least), eternity does manifest itself in historical process, the history of Israel and the unfolding of its theology being the elect vessel of that manifestation. The appropriateness of a historical-critical approach to the Old Testament, then, is simply that the Old Testament itself, *qua* sacred history, demands it and gives rise to it. The same can be said about the New Testament, in which the claim that God makes himself known supremely in the historical event of Easter demands of us a discrimination of the pre-Easter and post-Easter perspectives.

But once we have said as much as this, we have come full circle and have joined hands with the prohibition of Article 20 again. We are forbidden any presentation of this historical dialectic which supposes it incapable of yielding a meaningful revelation — whether in the interests of a sceptical debunking of the supposed revelation or in the interests of a return to pre-critical understandings of the Bible. We are, then, at one with the Tudor theologians in forbidding an interpretation which treats historical diversities, contrasts and conflicts as *repugnancies*. A term which should be banished for ever from the exegesis of Scripture is the word "contradiction", which bespeaks an ahistorical, two-dimensional understanding of the Scriptural texts that conceives of them all as synchronous and competing propositions, rather than dialectically successive and mutually implicating testimonies of God's unfolding self-disclosure. The modern tradition has been entirely wasted on us if we end up with as ahistorical a conception of scriptural revelation as we started with, but merely with the added presumption that we can make our choice between contrasting elements according to our own prejudices. What, for example are we to say about the degenerate liturgical habit of expurgating the Psalms of those elements which are "incompatible" with Jesus's command to forgive our enemies? Does it not express the idea that the Psalms, with their cries for vengeance, are liturgically contemporaneous with Jesus's words, and so in direct competition with them? Is it not the virtue of retaining these contrasts in our liturgy (however distasteful to our unreflective sensibilities) that it will prevent us from hearing even Jesus's words ahistorically, and from failing to comprehend how they came to be uttered, and so what they mean within the history of salvation? In such ways we see that the sense of Article 20, though formally seeming to oppose the whole enterprise of historical dialectic, must, at a deeper level, undergird it: and that historical interpretation collapses (as it has constantly done) into ahistorical repugnancies precisely when there is a failure of belief in the unity of God's disclosure through historical process. For it is not only "reading" that makes a presupposition of unity; "history" does, too.

And here we must venture a warning against some recent trends which have set out to recover the unity of the text of Scripture without, it would appear, grasping the nettle of finding the unity in the history behind Scripture. It is not enough to read the text of Scripture *as* a text, and look for the textual unity which properly belongs to it as such. That way lies the danger that we will treat of an abstraction: a "Scripture" which has been carefully lifted out of the history through which it came to be, and with which it seeks to put us in touch. History will be abandoned to the chaos which (it is presumed) the modern tradition has made it out to be. Unity will be located in a purely literary phenomenon, a text which is something of an artificial construct. To stress the unities of the text, *qua* text, may, of course, be very useful as a counterbalance to unliterary projects of dismemberment on the part of the old-style form- and source- critics. But if the end of the enterprise is not to discern a unifying purposiveness in reality, that is, a "history" which belongs to events and not merely to art, then its service to us is merely aesthetic.

With these considerations in mind, we return to the Articles on Scripture, and especially to Article 7, which deals with the oldest and most persistent challenge to the theologian to demonstrate the unity which lies behind the diversity and contrasts of historical revelation: the place of the Old Testament in the Christian Scriptures. This offers a test of our thesis that historical criticism of the Scriptures was evoked above all by the datum of the Scriptures themselves; for if this is so, we will expect to find, here more than anywhere else, anticipations of the insights which one associates with the modern tradition of reading.

The Article begins with a stress upon the unity of the Testaments, by denying the contention, (historically associated with the second-century gnostic Marcion, but also exercising an influence upon some groups within the Reformation) that "the Old Testament is contrary to the New".

Before we follow the criticism of this contention, let us remark upon its strengths. It was determined to be radically Christian, to take its stand on the revelation of God in Jesus Christ and nowhere else. It was suspicious of the claim that God gave the law to Moses on Sinai, that the word of the Lord came to Jeremiah or that the Lord had opened the Psalmist's lips. It took its bearings from the New Testament alone, because in it was to be found the apostolic witness to Jesus, whereas the law, the prophets and the writings, composed long before, could know nothing of him. But, of course, the apostolic witness to Jesus is full of references to the law, prophets and writings. In order to rid the church of the incubus of the Old Testament Marcion had had to excise large parts of the New. And this shows up the true character of the Marcionite proposal: it lacked a sense of historical depth which could see Jesus, as the apostles saw him, as the ultimate confirmation of the "sure mercies of David" and the promise of God to Abraham. The Jesus it could cope with was a mere abstraction. It was the great achievement of Luther, that in seeking to show up the centrality of Christ as a revelation of divine mercy, he never allowed the opposition between Moses and Christ to develop into a simplistic Marcionite refusal of the Old Testament, but held to the sharp historical dialectic in which Law and Gospel were both true manifestations of the one God.

Article 7, however, does not start where Luther starts, with the opposition of Law and Gospel, but with a much more Calvinist stress upon the unity of the divine revelation: "both in the Old and New Testament everlasting life is offered to mankind by Christ, who is the only mediator between God and man." The Old Testament always contains the message of Christ implicit within it, "Wherefore they are not to be heard which feign that the old fathers did look only for transitory promises." Certainly the Old Testament is full of these so-called "transitory promises" which relate only to the history of Israel and have no universal reference: a land, a king descended from David, an existence free from threat of war, a fruitful economy. But each of these local and limited hopes is made a vehicle by which something universal, looming on the horizon of the future, makes itself known. "They were reaching out", says the Epistle to the Hebrews (11:16) "for a better homeland, that is, a heavenly one." This general programme for the Christian reading of the Old Testament, uncontroversial in the Catholic West as in the Orthodox East, is open to a number of different exegetical interpretations. One might, for example, find in the Old Testament an extended *theophany*, which contains symbolic representations of heavenly and eternal realities: images of the divine Trinity, the Kingdom of God or the spiritual purity of the redeemed soul. Or one might find narrative types which anticipate the salvific rôle that is to be played by Christ, in Isaac, for example, the restored sacrifice, or in Joseph the pioneer of his people's journey, thus extending to the narrative elements the character of *prophecy*. Both these exegetical approaches were familiar enough to the Western church, but the English Reformers make no mention of them here. They point us, instead, to the character of the Old Testament as *law*, a move in a somewhat surprising direction given the remark about "promises" in the preceding sentence, and one which leaves a slight sense of hiatus in the text. But that move is not only characteristic of the Reformation as a whole, which developes its understanding of the Old Testament in response to Luther's treatment of Law and Gospel; it also shows a willingness to develop the general thesis of continuity in the direction of historical dialectic. For to speak of "law" is to speak not only of eternal realities, but of orders that are tied to particular societies at particular times; it is to speak of that which passes away, as well as that which endures.

The law of any society has two aspects. On the one hand, it is that which establishes and maintains order, and as such mediates the order of creation and establishes a relation between the life of society and the good for which mankind was created. On the other, it is not simply identical to the social good, but is in various respects arbitrary: societies are different from each other, and live under different pressures, with different capacities for organization and communication, different educational levels, different motivations. The law (even assuming that in every case it is wise and good law) will differ in accordance with differing social needs. It had been said consistently since the early fathers of the church that the religious law of ancient Israel was determined by its structure in salvation-history, as an order of sacraments which communicated the benefits of Christ yet to appear. In the middle ages an additional point was made: that the law of ancient Israel was determined by its contingent character as a society: by its social, educational, moral structure within history. These two elements of contingency in Old Testament law are recognized in the remark that "the law as touching ceremonies and rites, do (*sic*) not bind Christian men, nor the civil precepts thereof ought of necessity to be received in any commonwealth". Thus a division is set between the Christian era and the society to which the Old Testament (as law) bears witness. The dialectic of historical development is acknowledged. The order by which the social good was mediated in ancient Israel cannot claim us immediately, but is part of the historical dialectic through which the gospel of Christ was revealed. Yet this contingent social order was *also* a mediation of the universal good; to understand it is not enough to understand its contingency, but we must understand its relation to the universal good as well. Hence we detect also within this law a revelation of created order and the good to which all men are called, a "moral law" by which every human being is claimed and which belongs fundamentally to men's welfare. The theologian's task in expounding the Old Testament is to allow the contingent and the universal to emerge distinctly. If the *universal* does not shine through the contingent, then what is done is not theology, but only history: if the universal does not shine *through the contingent*, then what is done is bad theology, not founded in the narration of God's mighty deeds in saving-history, and so inadequately Christian.

The importance of the Old Testament to Christian faith lies in the history to which it bears witness — by which we mean not only the dramatic events of exodus, conquest and exile but also the institutional context which forms the fabric of Old Testament society: monarchy, temple and law. This history matters because it is the pre-history out of which was to arise the history of the Messiah. Through it we discern the end for which God created the world — the good for human existence, to which the economy of salvation is directed. The particular instruments do not bind us, not simply because time as such has moved on, but because God's time has moved on, and we stand the other side of the great climax towards which they tended. As we read the Old Testament we acknowledge the importance of all of it; yet we have to distinguish different ways in which it is important to us. And our key to that lies in the New Testament. Article 7, in using the threefold categorization of Old Testament law to bring out the continuity of the whole Scripture and the historical opposition of old and new, achieves very nearly a perfect balance.

5

THE CONCEALMENT OF CREATION
(Articles 9,10)

And now we reach a point where we can hardly help being uneasy.

Having said all they wish to say about the Scriptures, the Articles will turn to the doctrines of salvation; but before they do so they must pause to establish the doctrine which salvation presupposes, that of mankind's fall. This they describe, perfectly correctly, as "the fault and corruption of the nature of every man". But about the nature of man itself, that in which the fault and corruption resides, they have nothing to say. That mankind is the creature of God, made in God's image, set at the head of God's creation, a physical being with rational powers to understand and to rule the rest of creation and to worship God appropriately: these things are nowhere acknowledged in the Articles. But that is only an aspect of a larger omission, the doctrine of creation itself. In Article 1 God was described as "the maker and preserver of all things both visible and invisible"; and with that brief reference Cranmer and his successors said everything that they had to say about the creation of the world. Even the customary defence, that this doctrine was not at issue in the polemical situation in which they wrote, will not entirely serve to excuse this strange silence, since the continental Reformers had, indeed, found themselves arguing with the scholastic tradition on the nature of the image of God in man.

Their silence anticipates a much more widespread malaise which was to afflict the understanding of creation in later Protestant theology. In Lutheranism creation became assimilated to the law, and was consequently contrasted rather too sharply with the gospel. In continental Calvinism the doctrine was on the whole well taught; but in the Puritan Calvinism of the seventeenth century English-speaking world creation became assimilated to providence, and so changed its character completely. In Anglicanism the influence of Richard Hooker gave some aspects of the Thomistic understanding of creation a tenuous hold by way of the doctrine of Natural Law. But of all the elements in the rich Thomistic theology of creation which might have influenced our thinking, it can be argued that this was the least helpful one, in that it encouraged a narrower, humanistic conception of creation-order, restricted to the aspirations of the human will for self-fulfilment. So was the way prepared both for the subjective and moralistic consciences of the Caroline divines and for the behavioural social sciences of Hobbes and Locke. But which came first, Hooker or the humanistic concept of nature? Already there are anticipations of the latter before us in Article 9.

Our discomfort at this point, then, is not the well-known perturbation of moderns confronted with the strangeness of classical Christian perceptions, as it has been in previous Articles. It is the more surprising, and therefore the more unsettling, disturbance experienced by late moderns when confronting the roots of modernity. After all, in the more recent phases of the modern era we have not been without an interest in creation; the scientific character of our civilization has forced it upon theology as a topic of continuing importance. What the appearance of this hiatus right at the beginning of the modern period means for us is that our contemporary discussions spring from a break in the tradition. The first adventures in scientific thinking took place in a vacuum where the Christian doctrine of creation might have, but did not, control the direction in which these adventures proceeded. The most that can be said for the influence of the Reformation at large (the phrase is designed to allow a preeminent exception for Calvin) is that it facilitated the development of science negatively, by bringing into disrepute some earlier theologies of the world which conceded too little to the distance between the creature and the creator, and by putting nothing in their place. Instead of a strong recovery of the patristic *creatio ex nihilo*, what the Reformation as a whole offers us is a gap between God and the world, true, but one which permits of no ordered perceptions of the world, because it is characterized solely by sin and fallenness. The opposition of God and the world becomes swallowed up into the opposition of good and evil. Science, therefore, develops within the context of a world-view which understands nature apart from norms, and is idealist in its understanding of beauty and order. If we wish to understand the phenomenon of liberal Protestantism as it emerged in the nineteenth century, there is no better way than to ask what was bound to become of a Christianity shorn of the doctrine of creation, confronted with a self-confident and normless experimental science.

These observations, however, take us outside our scope, into the era of science, the seventeenth century and beyond. We need not wander so far to trace the damage done by a weak doctrine of creation. It is evident in the sixteenth century itself, as may be seen in what Article 9 makes of the Augustinian tradition of original sin.

The controversy between Pelagius and Saint Augustine, to which the Article refers in its first sentence, raised issues that sprang into prominence again in the course of the Reformation. The Edwardian form of the Article attributed Pelagian views to contemporary Anabaptists; but the original source of the concern was not in Anabaptist teachings but in the debate over justification with the Roman communion, as Article 2 of the Augsburg Confession makes clear. The question has continued in many Protestant eyes to determine the shape of the debate between Protestantism and Catholicism since. The belief of Pelagius, which led him into conflict with Augustine in the second decade of the fifth century A.D., was fashioned by his strong sense of individual moral responsibility. Each of us must take the blame for the wrong things we do and must shoulder the burden of moral resolution that will amend our lives. We should not attempt to blame our weakness on our "human nature", which was a perfectly good human nature when God gave it to us; if it is weak and enslaved to bad habits now, we have only ourselves to thank. The implication is that each of us began our lives equipped with a humanity that had no involvement with sin, and that the involvement which we now have has been picked up on the way. Each of us, as it were, began in his own Garden of Eden, with his own innocence. Adam's fall, the abuse of his free-will to rebel against the command of God, is the pattern for what each of us has done, the paradigm case for human wilfulness, the first of the long series, a series in which every individual human, at least every adult and morally responsible human, has followed him.

Augustine was sure that this was wrong. We do not each begin where Adam began; we begin where Adam left off. The fall of Adam was not simply a paradigm for the way all men fall. It was the determining factor that controlled what it has meant to be a human being ever since. In Pelagius's view it was possible (though very unlikely) that a new-born baby would never sin. Perhaps it would gasp once and die, before it had had a chance to look upon forbidden fruit. But for Augustine it was already too late for such hopes. The new-born child belonged to a *race* that lives under the effects of Adam's sin. It was a human being. No member of the fallen race, not even the youngest, could live as though the fall had not happened. This is the position that the Article intends to make its own when it begins: "Original sin standeth not in the following of Adam [that is, in imitating his example] as the Pelagians do vainly talk."

But as we notice how the Article proceeds, we cannot help becoming conscious of a gap between the Reformers and their model, a gap that is the more striking because it is unconscious: "but it is the fault and corruption of the nature of every man, that naturally is engendered of the offspring of Adam." The un-Augustinian note is struck by the word "every" — the Latin is *cuiuslibet* —, confirming that Cranmer means to say, not "mankind as a whole", but "each and every, considered individually". And this raises the question: what, then, does he mean by "nature"? And what does he mean by ascribing "fault and corruption" to nature as he construes it?

The issue between Pelagius and Augustine turned on whether "fallen humanity" was an individual or a collective attribute. "Human nature" for Augustine is something which we hold in common, a collective reality which has its own racial history and its own moral position, in which we, who participate in it, are inextricably involved. It fell "in Adam". We who are born into the race are born into a community of rebellion against God. The fault and corruption of our nature precede and determine our individual existences. All of this Augustine maintained in order to escape from the Pelagian sense of individual responsibility in which "nature" was *my* nature, the nature that came to existence with me at my birth and for whose defects only I, through my own choices and action, can be held to blame. But how, then, can Cranmer refer to the nature of *each* (*cuiuslibet*) man, without at least partly siding with Pelagius against Augustine? And if this *cuiuslibet* is taken seriously, what is the "fault and corruption" of the nature of *each* man? Not — for this would be straightforward Pelagianism — the damage that he has himself done to it by his own irresponsible choices. The Article is devoted to affirming the conception of an "original" or "birth sin", which must be predicated of each and every human prior to any choices he may make. But if the nature we are talking about is *individual* nature, and if it was corrupt from birth, then we must conclude that it was never anything other than corrupt. The notion of an "original righteousness", to which the Article alludes later in the first sentence, can make sense only if it is predicated of *collective human nature*. It defends the anti-Pelagian position against a collapse into Manichaeism. It asserts that the humanity which God made was "very good", that the created order had no blemish or fault, and that the fault and corruption of human nature is by no means a defect in God's workmanship. Augustine's belief in a real human nature as such, and not simply a multitude of individual human natures, was the critical platform from which he could reject Pelagian individualism on the one hand without rejecting creation on the other. "Nature" was never evil for Augustine, only the fault (*vitium*) which man inflicted on nature. And in Cranmer we see, on the one hand, a silence about creation, and, on the other, a suspiciously individualistic treatment of human nature. Must we not be anxious that the first steps into Manichaeism are here being taken? taken?

But the word *cuiuslibet* is, after all, a short rope to hang anyone on. We had better follow Cranmer further.

Original sin is "the fault and corruption of the nature of every man, that naturally is engendered of the offspring of Adam". For Augustine, the descent of every human being from Adam was the necessary correlate to the unity and solidarity of the human race. Why is the human race one? Because it is descended from one ancestor. This association of ideas is undoubtedly difficult for us, since we are no longer accustomed to read the creation stories of Genesis as historical narratives. It may, however, be said to be our problem rather than Augustine's, since the notion of a unitary human race is one that we still cling to more passionately than ever, and the actual steps by which the first appearance of this human race occurred on earth are shrouded now, as much as ever, in scientific ignorance and semi-mythical speculation. If we can believe in the unity of the human race without believing in the descent from a single ancestor, we are free to do so — though not free to ignore the fact that the humanity of any individual human being was given him by way of human parents, a matter that is of great importance in understanding the human race as one race even across the gulf of generations. For Augustine, then, the force of his assertion of common ancestry lay in the solidarity of the race and the unity of human nature. He developed (as is well known) a speculative train of thought about how the process of generation served to transmit original sin from parent to child, a train of thought which is universally admitted to have been unsatisfactory as a theory of sin, though it showed startling insight into certain aspects of sexual psychology. Such speculation was not, however, the heart of his account of original sin, but was merely intended to give the central contention some elaboration and development.

And Cranmer? There is nothing yet that entitles us to draw a conclusion; the reference to Adam might be taken precisely as an attempt to reintroduce the notion of a universal human nature — as the reference to "original righteousness" suggests. But we may at least be anxious lest, with the notions of created order and a universal human nature missing, there will follow also a depreciation not only of human nature (considered individualistically) but also of the natural process of generation, another trait of Manichaeism which Augustine was concerned to avoid.

"Whereby man is very far gone from original righteousness, and is of his own nature inclined to evil." Augustine, as we have said, did not like to say that human nature (or indeed any nature) was evil; though he would say that there was "evil in it", as well as saying that it was "corrupted" and "faulted". Occasionally, when he did go so far as to say that it was evil, he would add: "but not *an* evil". The expression "of his own nature inclined to evil" is not unthinkable in Augustine's pages, but it lacks the kind of safeguard that we would expect to find there. The reference to original righteousness, on the other hand, and to a collective "man", is hopeful and in keeping with the Augustinian conception of a created human nature that was good before its corruption. Yet the Latin text unfortunately does not create the same impression on this point as the English: the collective "man" is missing, the phrase *cuiuslibet hominis* is remembered as the assumed subject of the clause beginning *qua fit ut ab originali justitia*, so that *sua natura*, "of his own nature", takes on a more individualist sense: *each* man is, by his own *individual* nature, inclined to evil. Unhappily, this reading is the one which most naturally prepares the way for the last words of the sentence: "so that the flesh lusteth always contrary to the spirit". It is at this point that our suspicions, which have been until now no more than uneasy presentiments, begin to find some confirmation.

We notice, first, an exegetical mishap, for which Cranmer can hardly be blamed, but which is revealing, nevertheless, of the way his thought turns. He alludes to Gal. 5:17, "The flesh lusts against the Spirit, and the Spirit against the flesh." The universal consensus of modern exegetes gives an initial upper case to "Spirit", understanding Paul to refer to the Holy Spirit and to its contest with "the flesh", which is to say, the impulses of unredeemed human nature; whereas Cranmer, on the most natural reading, takes "flesh" and "spirit" to be competing parts of the human soul. There is nothing especially ominous in this mishap. Augustine did likewise, even when he was directly attacking the Manichaean use of the Galatians text to decry the body. The question, rather, is how Cranmer comes to find in the moral struggle which the text describes a demonstration of *original sin*. To be involved in moral struggle, to find the flesh contrary to Spirit (whether with upper or with lower case) is not a condition of sin, but of temptation. Should someone offer the defence that temptation could not assume this painful and disruptive form in a humanity not tainted by original sin, we may agree that that is very true; nevertheless, the Article proceeds immediately to declare that "it deserveth God's wrath and damnation", something which we may not say about temptation. Original sin deserves judgement; all are involved in original sin; all are consequently tempted by the conflict of flesh and spirit; but that does not mean that temptation deserves judgement, nor that it is identical with original sin.

From his use of the Galatians text we begin to discern what Cranmer conceives original sin to be. It is the conception of late Augustinianism, not of Augustine. Original sin is the inner evil-in-potential, the perverse striving within our thoughts and heart, to which each of us can testify in honest introspection. It is the subjective evil inclination which we find within ourselves, a seed in the active soul from which all kinds of wicked acts spring forth, a constitutional fault within our agency. It comes to us by inheritance, which is to say that it is a seed within a seed, a spring of evil wrapped up in the very spring of human existence. Such is the subjective and pessimistic conception to which the notion of original sin is reduced when it loses its ground in an objective creation-order containing a collective human nature. Dominated by the antithesis of potential and actual, it absorbs even temptation into the generalized bias towards evil which it has described as original sin, and so severs the connexion between temptation and innocence. For if it is true that every man who is tempted is, in one sense, *already* guilty by his membership of the sinful race, it is also true that he is in another sense (relative to that particular evil) quite innocent — a point which has great importance for the sinlessness of Christ, who, as Heb. 4:15 would tell us, "was tempted like us in all things, yet without sin." To anticipate for a moment: it would seem to be a significant admission that at the beginning of Article 15 Cranmer finds himself unable to quote that text without emending it.

The second and third sentences of Article 9 reject one form of perfectionism: belief in the immediate liberation of the regenerate from original sin. To this theme the Articles will return, and we with them. Our interest now is confined to the way in which the concept of original sin is developed further by the use of two more Pauline texts. We are taken to Rom. 8:8, where the apostle says that the "mind of the flesh" (*phronema sarkos*) is death; and then to Rom. 7:7, where, alluding to the tenth command of the Decalogue, he writes: "I could not have known what sin was, except through the law. I would not have known what lust was if the law had not said, 'Thou shalt not lust'. Now, the Article supposes that these two texts and Galatians 5:17 all refer to the same thing. The contrariety of flesh and spirit is the same as the mind of the flesh, and they two are the same as the lust which the Decalogue prohibits; and all alike have "the nature of sin".

But the context of the expression *phronema sarkos* in Rom. 8 belies its identification with the struggle of flesh and spirit in Galatians. For

although the contrast is made, once again, between the flesh and the
Spirit, Saint Paul is now talking about those who "live according to"
the flesh and the Spirit, and "set their minds on" (*phronousin*) the flesh
or the Spirit. The R.S.V. translates *to phronema tēs sarkos* as "the
mind set upon" the flesh — a good rendering (better than any of those
that the Article finds itself unable to choose among) suggesting, as is
appropriate, a settled moral attitude. Here, in other words, Paul is not
talking about temptation, but about decision and policy. Equally
inappropriate is the use of Rom. 7:7 to support the claim that desire
alone constitutes individual sin. (Cranmer might equally well, and
equally inappropriately, have referred to Christ's teaching that
whoever looks on a woman to lust after her has committed adultery in
his heart.) We cannot deny that there *is* such a thing as sinful
entertainment of desire — to which the command "Thou shalt not
covet" is directed. Nevertheless, this sinful entertainment of desire
must be properly distinguished from simple temptation, in which one
struggles against improper desire. That distinction is obscured by our
Article when it brings Romans 7:7 into conjunction with the verse
from Galatians 5.

What does this criticism of the most unsuccessful of the Thirty-Nine
Articles amount to? Not, certainly, that Cranmer was a Manichaean.
But he represents a theological culture which was careless about
defining itself against tendencies towards Manichaeism, which did not
view the fact of moral struggle hopefully, as a sign that God's Spirit
was at work combating the indiscipline of the fleshly instincts, but
gloomily, as a proof that the moral battle was lost before it was
begun, the citadel of the inner man having fallen to the possession of
the enemy even before he could be conscious of it. And this because it
had lost its hold on a strong doctrine of creation, the belief in the
primordial goodness of all nature and the reality of corporate human
solidarity, which had enabled Augustine to find a position that was
neither Pelagian nor Manichaean. To expose this weakness at such
length is neither captious nor carping; for it is important to identify
the theological structure which prevailed in the century before the
scientific revolution first began to make thought "modern". The
hidden liaison between Manichaeism and experimental science,
manifest as early as the fourteenth century, is one of the most
important formative influences to shape the modern world. In Article
9 we see a theological culture that has expelled the Pelagian devil, and
is now swept and garnished, defenceless against the stronger devils of
seventeenth-century scepticism.

More broadly we may say that Augustine's doctrine of original sin
was capable of development in either of two directions. The theme of
genetic inheritance invited the understanding of sin as individual

potentiality for evil; the theme of corporate solidarity suggested an understanding of it as community in actual guilt. It has been fateful for Western thought that mediaeval and Reformation understandings took the first way rather than the second. Further down the road that Cranmer took there lay a community of psychological accounts of innate evil, such as Kierkegaard's famous conception of *Angst*, which seems to combine the disadvantages of a Manichaean evil principle and a Pelagian individual fall. The other road, less trodden in the West, leads to some modern attempts, prompted by the social sciences, to account for evil in terms of the controlling structures of society. Is it too simple to suggest that a satisfactory account of the immanence of evil will lie at the point where these two roads meet up again? The value and fascination of Augustine's doctrine consisted in its attempt, however unclear, to embrace the complementary aspects of human evil, the inward experience of the evil inclination and the actual moral offence of our shared human existence, encouraging each aspect to interpret the other.

Commentators on Article 10 are inclined to observe that the title "Of Free Will" is somewhat unsuitable. It may be so; but it is very revealing, because what this Article talks about is what the Reformers almost all meant by free-will, and we will not understand their debates on the subject unless we observe the fact. The loss of free-will is simply the incapacity of fallen man to "turn and prepare himself by his own natural strength and good works, to faith and calling upon God."

Absence of freedom is a condition of the fall, and not a condition of creation. So we are instructed in the first sentence, derived by the Elizabethans from the Confession of Würtemberg. To compare the debates of the Reformation with later, seventeenth- and eighteenth-century debates, ostensibly on the same subject, is to be struck by a great contrast. In the later period those who defended the freedom of the will (called "Arminians", an inexact but convenient title) sought to establish the notion of an act of will as causeless and unnecessitated, a radical new beginning to a chain of causation; and those who attacked it (called "Calvinists" irrespective of their more general theological affiliations) criticized the possibility of such a causeless event in principle. The debate was, in fact, about contingency and necessity within creation. But among the Reformers nobody (and certainly not Calvin!) had questioned that Adam was created free. The debate was, in fact, about something else; it was a more theological and less philosophical debate, an adjunct to the doctrine of justification.

What was in question was our capacity to take an independent moral initiative. Mankind was lacking, not in the capacity to make free decisions as such, but the capacity to make decisions which would affect in any way his moral standing under God's judgment. This, of course, was assumed in the gospel message itself, that God had to take the initiative in sending his Son to earth to redeem mankind. But then the question arose: granted that the deed of salvation, by which mankind was redeemed, was one that only God could effect, what about each individual's *belief* in that deed? Belief is, to a certain extent, a moral act and turns on our moral disposition. Must we not say that it is up to men whether they believe or not? Plainly in one sense we must say this, since belief is a decision of man for which he is responsible, as he is for all his other acts. We would be wrong to suggest that human beings come to believe in Christ only by the *suspension* of a capacity which they otherwise exercise. In that case, as we would now say, belief would be "inauthentic". So much may reasonably be said — but it is possible to be too impressed by this power of human decision and to forget the context within which it must be exercised. For the act of belief, too, can occur only as God evokes it: no one can say "Jesus is Lord", says Saint Paul, except through the Holy Spirit (1 Cor. 12:3).

In reading Article 9 we became aware that we stood on the threshold of the scientific age, the age in which mechanical conceptions of causation supplanted the idea of an order of creation. In reading Article 10 we must remember that we have not crossed that threshold. We are not to conceive the grace of God in a deterministic and causal way, as later generations were to do and as, indeed, early Calvinist determinism was already tending to do. If we do so, we will find ourselves forced into the impossible either-or of radical voluntarism and determinism which rendered later discussions sterile from a theological point of view. In the Tudor period it was still possible to pose the question without evoking chains of causation. Prevenient grace ("by Christ", Cranmer adds, like a good Reformer, eager to avoid the purely providential conception of grace which separated it from the history of salvation) evokes a good will. And we would do as well to choose an analogy from the moral influence which operates between persons — the way in which another person's radiant goodness calls out the best in us, another person's love makes us love, another person's learning incites the desire to study — as to reach for concepts of mechanical causation and necessity. Such analogies are, of course, themselves too weak — how could the moral influence of another human being be sufficient to suggest the redemptive power of God? — and to cling exclusively to them would lead us to the sentimentally debilitated deity of romanticism. Nevertheless, they suggest better than a row of dominoes can ever do how it can be that our wills are actually set free by an influence which bears upon us from outside. The intention of avoiding mechanistic conceptions was actually clearer in the Edwardian Articles, where our Article 10 (Cranmer's ninth) was followed by another Article, "Of Grace", to which we have already alluded, where Cranmer wrote: "Although, those that have no will to good things, he maketh them to will, and those that would evil things, he maketh them not to will the same: yet nevertheless he enforceth not the will." The removal of that Article marks the growth of Calvinist influence at the beginning of Elizabeth's reign.

"The grace of God by Christ preventing us:" It acts on us first, producing in us a good will; and then it goes on working with us, because there is never a time when we can become independent of God for our response to him. Thus grace is (to use the technical terms associated with scholasticism) "prevenient" and "cooperative". It is satisfying to contemplate this moment in the career of the English Reformation when it drew on the tradition of Saint Thomas to ward off the influence of late-mediaeval voluntarism on the one hand and early Calvinist predestinarianism on the other.

6

SALVATION IN CHRIST
(Articles 11—18)

The theme of the central block of Articles is set by the last sentence of Article 18 — which echoes St. Peter's great statement at Acts 4:12, "There is no other name under heaven given to men whereby we must be saved." The theme is salvation in Christ, and in Christ alone. It is an exclusive theme, rejecting the assumption of a liberal pluralism that any creed will serve us provided that we are scrupulous and consistent in our adherence to it. The Christian church has always made this exclusive claim, and that is why the status of other religious professions has always been something of a theological problem. Not that Christians have usually wished to exercise coercive methods to eradicate or oppress other religions. There have been periods and movements in which this was the case — the conversion of Northern Eurpoe, for example, was achieved with a very free use of the sword — but generally speaking, Christians, even in rather sanguinary periods of history, have felt that there were good reasons, arising from the character of Christian faith itself, for distrusting this mode of proceeding. Thus Christianity in the West has fostered a *political* organization that was liberal and pluralist, while remaining *theologically* exclusive.

What is the root of this exclusivism? Cranmer, following the text from Acts, exposes it as a Christological exclusiveness rather than a philosophical one or an ecclesiological one. It arises from the uniqueness of Jesus of Nazareth, the anointed of God and the Son of

Man, the representative not only of Jewry but of all mankind before the throne of God. A theology which wishes to understand Jesus as the New Testament understands him will need to take up the unfashionable cross of defending the exclusiveness of the apostles' claims for him, counter to all the prejudices and inclinations of our age. Yet in doing so, it will need to clarify where this exclusiveness really belongs. It will have no truck with other claims to exclusiveness which sometimes seem to ride upon its back: the irreplaceability of a theological tradition, for example, or of a church institution, or of a cultural form. And in pursuing its criticism of these false claimants to the universal throne of Christ, it will probably find itself no less open (dare one say, even more open?) to genuine instruction from other religious world-views than would an abstractly eclectic universalism.

Turning back from Article 18 to the seven Articles which precede it, we explore under two broad headings what it means to be saved "in Christ". The two headings are Justification and Predestination, both of them characteristic themes of the Reformation period, both derived from the concerns and debates of mediaeval theologians. The doctrine of justification is concerned with how we participate in the *righteousness* of Christ, the doctrine of predestination with how we participate in the *eternal purpose* which the Father has for his Son. The two themes, justification and predestination, speak of our salvation in Christ, one from the perspective of Christ's historical existence, the other from the perspective of his eternal relationship with the Father.

The concept of justification has been so closely associated with the Reformation that we could easily overlook, were it not for the promptings of recent late-mediaeval scholarship, the extent to which the questions of the sixteenth century had their roots in mediaeval theology. The achievement of the Reformers was not to raise the question of justification for the first time, but to handle it in a new way, and so to give new answers. The question itself was the fruit of the Augustinian tradition of thinking about divine grace. More fundamentally, of course, it is the fruit of the exegesis of Saint Paul; but the direction which that exegesis took, and the prominence assumed within it by the question of justification, were determined by the general Augustinian problematic: what is the significance of human moral achievement in relation to the grace of God which precedes it, gives rise to it, accompanies it, and crowns it? But the Augustinian tradition treated the question in abstraction from salvation-history, as an issue concerning God and the individual human agent alone. The point at which the Reformers, and especially Luther, reinterpreted the question, and recovered a dimension of the biblical treatment which had been lost, was in reconnecting it with Christology and bringing it under the scope of the thesis, "only the name of Jesus Christ, whereby men must be saved". Viewed from the psychological and ethical perspective of the mediaeval discussions, the Reformers' positions on justification have an undoubtedly gaunt, even inhumane appearance. But it is the artificially narrow perspective that is at fault. The compelling force of the Reformers' answers is that they reintroduce the forgotten middle-term in the relation of God and the soul: the effective agent of God and the representative of man, Jesus Christ, whose work of salvation is complete and decisive, the last word to which nothing can be added, an achievement within time which yet towers over time and which can never, therefore, be a proposition to which we answer, a thesis to which we add an antithesis, but is already proposition and answer, thesis and antithesis, all in one.

At the centre, then, of the Articles on justification is a Christological Article (15) from which the section as a whole gains its orientation. It asserts that Christ is the one sinless man, unique in his sinlessness, and therefore unique in his capacity to represent true humanity. Not even the redeemed can stand where he stands; for although, in one sense, to be among the redeemed is nothing other than to stand where he stands, the redeemed stand there only "in him", not in themselves. For them to be sinless means to be represented in the humanity of another; for him to be sinless is to represent the humanity of others in his own. Around this cardinal and irreversible relationship of all mankind to this man, the characteristic Reformation denials of human righteousness and works revolve; apart from it they are unintelligible. This is the first point which the Elizabethan revisers, in words taken from the Würtemberg Confession, set before us in Article 11: "We are accounted righteous before God, only for the merit of our Lord and Saviour Jesus Christ, by faith, and not for our own works or deservings."

Two elements in that statement demand our special attention. First, it is for *the merit of our Lord and Saviour Jesus Christ* that we are accounted righteous. This establishes the ethical basis of justification. There is no suggestion that goodness and moral integrity do not matter. God has never ceased to be pleased by the righteousness of mankind. He is pleased with the one man who is truly righteous, Jesus. And when Jesus's righteousness begins to be seen in his followers, God is still pleased with it. Article 12, which was wisely added by Parker to establish the positive doctrine of good works which was left merely implicit in Cranmer's denials, declares that "good works which are the fruits of faith . . . are pleasing and acceptable to God in Christ" — the last two words of that quotation being the key to the whole. But the point is that such good works are by no means "our own". They are ours, of course, in the sense that they *become* ours, that it is *our* lives, loves and characters that become possessed by the life, love and character of Jesus and set free for God. But they are not ours in the sense that they originate with us — not even, as we shall see, "after" justification. They "spring out necessarily of a true and lively faith" — which is to say, they are the effect of our being united with Christ in faith. The Reformers' doctrine of justification, then, is a doctrine of the believer's moral union with Christ — an attack on the ethical individualism which characterized even the most anti-Pelagian of mediaeval treatments and a reassertion of the great New Testament themes of mankind's double representation, "in Adam" and "in Christ".

In the second place, it is said that *we are accounted righteous before God* for the merit of our Lord and Saviour Jesus Christ. What is the meaning of that "accounting", which stands in such sharp contrast to the factitive sense of justification as "making righteous" which prevails in mediaeval discussions? Why should the Reformers not say simply that God *makes* us righteous in Christ, and does their insistence on a "juridical" or "imputed" righteousness not expose them to the charge that they no longer believe that the moral renewal of mankind is essential to salvation? Of course, it exposes them to the *charge*, and it would be futile to deny that Protestant understandings of justification have sometimes strayed off in that direction. Nevertheless, there is a matter of importance wrapped up in that metaphor of "accounting", a metaphor which, after all, is used in this connexion by Saint Paul. It defends the finality of God's decision in the resurrection of Christ. God having raised up the righteous representative and set him on his right hand, what remains for him to do? Shall we say that he has many further tasks ahead of him, the making of numerous believers righteous? Shall we say that with only *one* man yet exalted to the throne of God, the redeeming work is hardly begun? Shall we say that with the Second Person home and dry, the Third Person has still to run his race? No, we may say none of these things. We must say that all is finished and complete. The sanctification of the many can do no more than realize the implications of what has already been accomplished. The coming of the Spirit to struggle with the flesh is simply a communication of the triumph that is won for all time. The doctrine of representation permits us to say no less and no more. What God does for the individual believer, then, is not a new and different work, a further "making righteous", but an application of the one complete work, a "counting" of this believer into the righteous Kingdom already established and in place. In saying that we are *counted* righteous, the Reformers did not challenge the link between salvation and wholeness; they challenged the restriction of salvation to the sphere of the individual soul. We cannot comprehend justification in terms of what God does for each soul; for what transpires within that private sphere is but the expression of a public work upon the widest cosmic front already achieved: the redemption of the human race.

In the light of these assertions, provided largely by the Elizabethan revisers, we can approach with more sympathy the four denials (13—16) taken verbatim from the Edwardian Articles. They concern congruent merit, works of supererogation, the sinlessness of the redeemed and the refusal of post-baptismal repentance. The four amount in effect to three (since the last two are really one) and have a common theme: they deny *independence* to the individual believer over against what God has done for him in Christ. They deny that he can make an independent *contribution* to his justification, that he can *improve* on it by going beyond what is implicit in it, and that he can have so *possessed* it as no longer to be dependent upon divine mercy. Because the first is in some ways the most difficult, we take them in reverse order.

The relationship between the believer and the one sinless representative of mankind is a relationship of complete dependence. In him we are acceptable and accepted; apart from him we are not acceptable and not accepted. This relationship is the beginning and end of our justification. It does not change. At all times in our lives, even when the Holy Spirit is bringing his life to fruitful effect in our lives, we are dependent upon him as sinners upon the sinless one. Article 15 rejects any conception of justification as an *achieved possession within our individual past histories*, an event on which we can count in such a way that we are no longer dependent as we once were dependent. When we speak of justification as finished and accomplished, we certainly should not mean that it is finished and accomplished in *our* lives — rather, that it is finished and accomplished in world-history with the death and resurrection of Christ. The conception of justification in purely biographical terms, as an item within the personal history of the individual with God, must necessarily lead either to a weakening of the concept altogether or to a perfectionism which (as Article 16 makes clear) has fanatical and tyrannical possibilities. Precisely because the death and resurrection of Christ is the one decisive climax of redemption-history, it stands in a uniform relation to all other moments of time. The individual biography moves, not in an upward curve away from the resurrection of Christ as a starting point, but in a circle around it, always in the same relation to it. Does this mean that there is no concept of Christian progress, no way in which individual biography, too, may reflect the imprint of a once-for-all redemption? Certainly it may, as we shall have cause to notice again when we consider the meaning of baptism. But when we refer to justification we do not *refer* to this biographical shape, to the moment of conversion or healing, to the growth in maturity or whatever; these are merely the signs which point to that other and prior achievement, the death and resurrection of Christ, upon which we are always, from beginning to end, dependent.

The correspondence of the righteousness of the believer to the righteousness of Christ implies the union of the one life with the other; it is not simply a matter of discrete duties or obligations, itemized acts of obedience or charity, a tally of external points of conformity which, once achieved, can be left behind in pursuit of some further good which lies outside the righteousness of Christ. Article 14 rejects any concept of justification which is not totalistic, which has narrowed its scope merely to some part of what we are to do. To be justified in Christ is to be dependent upon him for everything we are, become and achieve; it is to have an indebtedness that is coextensive with life itself, and which leaves us no scope for a truly independent initiative. The conception of "voluntary works besides, over and above, God's commandments" is that of a will which is somehow set free from the grace of God in Christ, which is able to cooperate with God on equal terms and respond to his goodness with our own. It is a natural fruit of mediaeval voluntarism, in which divine and human agents alike are seen as "causes", and in which the pinnacle of freedom is to be a cause uncaused. Into such a conception the traditional defence of monasticism, in terms of obedience to "evangelical counsels" which are not commands, fitted comfortably; and in rejecting the one the Reformers were bound to reject the other also. Whether they might have found a better way of reading the distinction between command and counsel had they looked for one, is a question we need not settle.

These two denials, of a biographical concept of justification and of an independent responsiveness to divine grace, both converge to motivate the denial of congruent merit in the Article "Of works before justification".

We notice, first of all, that it is about works *before* justification — not, that is, with the virtues of rank unbelievers, but with the possibility of a contribution to the event of justification itself. About the virtues of unbelievers nothing further will be said than has already been said in Article 10. Here we have to do with the one who is coming to belief, responding to "the grace of God by Christ preventing us", and the question is whether God, in conferring justification upon such a one, *himself* responds in any sense to the believer's response to prevenient grace. To this the Reformers reply that there is no element of response from the divine side to human initiative — not even the loosely conceived response of "appropriateness" (congruity) as opposed to "desert" (condignity). We notice, secondly, that it is about *works* before justification, and whether they are pleasing to God. To this the Reformers reply that they are not pleasant to God but have the nature of sin.

Here we become conscious of the constraints imposed by the mediaeval terms in which the discussion was conducted. It is perfectly clear why the Reformers had to reject the conception of congruent merit in justification. It was built upon a biographical notion of justification as an event in the believer's life, and upon a concept that individual human acts, treated in abstraction from the lives of which they form a part, could be the objects of divine favour or disfavour. What Cranmer needed to say was that neither the term "works" nor the term "before" was appropriate to the discussion. There is no "before justification" in a believer's life, since justification is the death and resurrection of Christ which long precedes his first thoughts of God. And there is no question of individual "works" being either pleasing or displeasing to God in isolation from the human agents who perform them. But instead of saying that, Cranmer merely denied the proposition about congruent merit in the terms in which it was put, and so gave rise to unnecessary offence in the minds of many who have failed to see what was really at issue. He appears to say simply that God looks on good deeds as sinful if they are not performed by believers — a curious attribution of arbitrary wilfulness to the divine, itself reminiscent of late-mediaeval voluntarism. Thus Cranmer failed quite to lay the mediaeval ghosts to rest, and they have continued to live their shadow-life, both among Protestants at large and among the Anglicans who looked specifically to him for guidance. It is perhaps not surprising that, with only the stark denial of Article 13 to offset it, the idea that God looks with favour on those who do what in them lies has had a lively and abiding presence in post-Reformation Anglicanism.

Predestination, like justification, was a theme of mediaeval theology, rooted in the same Augustinian tradition of thought about grace. Here, too, the Reformation instinct was to recover the connexion with Christology; but that instinct was in general less clear and much less effective in this doctrine than in the doctrine of justification. Before the Reformation began and in its early dawn, the classic Augustinian doctrine of predestination, which had provided the basis for mediaeval discussions, came under attack from the libertarian thought of the Renaissance; so that the first impulse of the early Reformers was to defend it. This polarization of the alternatives made the task of reworking the doctrine on a Christological foundation the more difficult. What was bequeathed to subsequent ages as "Calvinism" was, in effect, the Augustinian tradition, the common possession of the mediaeval schools, handed on to the modern age with only minor developments. In Cranmer's seventeenth Article, however, we see an attempt at a reformulation on Christological lines — an unprepossessing composition in many respects, lacking the clarity of Calvinist formulations and sometimes wearing the appearance of evasiveness. It does not achieve its Christological emphasis decisively, and moves in the right direction as much by what it refuses to say as by what it actually does say. Nevertheless, for all its tentative and unfinished character, it deserves to be thought of as a minor doctrinal landmark, an indication of how the Reformation might have achieved consistency with itself more effectively than in fact it did. Had Cranmer's line been followed rather than Calvin's, the succeeding centuries might have been spared the futile antagonism of determinist and voluntarist doctrines, or (if the dawn of Natural Science had made that arid deliberation inescapable) might at least have seen theology able to transcend it.

"Predestination to life is the everlasting purpose of God, whereby (before the foundations of the world were laid) he hath constantly decreed . . . to deliver . . . those whom he hath chosen in Christ . . . and to bring them by Christ to everlasting salvation . . ." The key to the doctrine as Cranmer see it lies in the two phrases "everlasting purpose" and "chosen in Christ". Predestination, like justification, is salvation in Christ; but where justification associates us with the righteousness of Christ manifest in his human life, predestination associates us with the eternal relation between the Son and the Father before all time. Who was the object of God's glad goodwill before the foundations of the world were laid? The one who could say, "I will tell of the decree of the Lord. He said to me, 'You are my son, today I have begotten you. Ask of me and I will make the nations your heritage'" (Ps. 2:7f). When we speak of man's salvation as "predestined", we are saying that the whole history of creation and salvation springs out of the eternal love which the Father bears to the Son, the love whereby he is resolved to give him a heritage, to make him "the first-born of many brethren" (Rom. 8:29). The phrase "chosen in Christ" is not to be understood as though *we* were chosen and *he* was merely the instrument by which our choosing was given effect. We are chosen in him, because *he* is the chosen one, the eternal object of the Father's good pleasure. Just as our justification means our participation in his righteousness, so our predestination, our "election", means our participation in his position as the object of the Father's favour from eternity.

Predestination, then, is a formal way of expressing the truth that the reality behind mankind's salvation is the eternal relation of the Father, the Son and the Holy Spirit within the Godhead. The doctrine of predestination underlines the denial of a purely economic trinitarianism.

The "economy" of creation and redemption is not the ultimate reality, which occasions the emergence of the Father, the Son and the Holy Spirit. Rather, the relation of the three, that the Father bestows his Spirit upon his Son in love and approval, constitutes the fundamental reality of the universe, and the history of creation and salvation is an expression of that relation, as we, created through the Son, are drawn by the Spirit to be the community of the Son's glorious Kingdom. "Ask of me, and I will make the nations your heritage," says the Father to his Son. What we see in history is the fulfilment of that eternal promise. We sometimes say that Jesus is called "elect" because he fulfils the election of Israel. It would be better to say that Israel is elect because it was allowed to anticipate the election of the Messiah. The revelation of God's eternal relation with his Son at a particular point in history was given an anticipatory and prophetic foreshadowing in the love which he bore for Israel, calling it his "Son". In listing the election privileges of Israel, St. Paul, at Rom. 9:44ff., writes: "They are Israelites, and to them belong the sonship, the glory, the covenant, the giving of the law, the worship, and the promises; to them belong the patriarchs, and" — concluding with the greatest mark of their status as the chosen people — "from their race, according to the flesh, is the Christ."

The distinctiveness of Cranmer's approach stands out when we lay this Article alongside chapter three of the Westminster Confession of Faith (1647).[1] (I take this document as marking the highest achievement of seventeenth-century Calvinism in the English church. The movement towards it can be seen in the Lambeth Articles of 1595 and the Irish Articles of 1615.)

That chapter expresses very well — albeit with seventeenth-century emphases — the classic doctrine of predestination which had its origins in the later writings of Saint Augustine and was finally given new currency by Calvin. There are three points in particular which distinguish the contents of that chapter from what we read in Cranmer's Article:

First, it is understood as a part of the general theistic content of the doctrines of God and creation, not as part of the doctrines of the Trinity and salvation. Chapter 3 of the Westminster Confession comes after Chapter 2, on God, and before Chapters 4 and 5, on Creation and Providence. It begins with the general assertion of §1, that God's eternal decrees govern whatever happens in the world, though in such a way that "liberty" and "contingency" are attributed to secondary causes; and it proceeds with the caution of §2, warning us against understanding this merely in terms of foreknowledge. Only then does it speak of predestination to life and foreordination to death, so that

[1] See Appendix 2

this decree is seen to be an instance of the more general principles that apply to God's governance of the world.

Secondly, it teaches the so-called "double decree", foreordination to death as well as predestination to life. This is a necessary corollary from the starting point in the doctrines of God and creation; for if, as has just been maintained, whatever happens happens because God makes it happen, it must follow that if anybody goes to hell, he goes there because God has made him go there. This gives a somewhat ambiguous aspect to creation, which can no longer be understood entirely positively in terms of God's sheer gift of being and life, but must have a negative aspect as well.

Thirdly, it teaches that the predestining decree is individual and particular. Certain angels and men, "particularly and unchangeably designed" (§4), are destined for these two ends. Thus the fundamental reality to which God's creation gives expression is the reality of individuals with fixed destinies. The drama of fall and salvation is understood as a "means" to accomplish these individually determined ends. The two great representatives of mankind, Adam and Christ, are introduced into God's purposes only in order to effect decisions about individuals that have been made logically prior to them. So one is saved or lost *before* one is a member either of Adam fallen or of Christ exalted.

Now let us compare this with what Cranmer wrote: —

First of all, the number: it is Article 17. It does not come at the beginning, with the doctrines of God and creation, but is among the Articles on salvation. For Cranmer this doctrine is about our salvation, and not part of the general theistic understanding of how a transcendent God directs contingent events.

Secondly, the Article does not speak of the double decree. This silence is emphasized by its peculiar shape. "Predestination to life is the everlasting purpose of God," it begins; and we naturally await a balancing sentence, "Foreordination to death . . ." etc. But it never comes. Cranmer will not say that there *is* such a thing as foreordination to damnation, but only that belief in such does exist and that the devil can make use of it. The point at issue here is that the classic doctrine has undertaken to speak of God's eternal purposes independently of the revelation of God in Jesus, on the basis of a concern which is purely theistic. The classic doctrine asks: how can an omnipotent and transcendent divinity live in the same universe with a world of free agents? Its answer cannot pass the test which must be applied to all theological utterances: do they show us the same God that is revealed to us in Christ? For the God who made the heavens and the earth and fixed the bounds of history is no other God than the one who showed himself, as he is, in Jesus. That consideration makes it impossible to believe in the double decree — at any rate, if it is understood as a doctrine about *creation*. God did not make beings in order to curse them. There is a curse, certainly, which God pronounces upon man's sin, and that means that there is the real possibility of God's pronouncing final judgement against any man; but even that curse and that judgement are a sign of God's goodwill towards the universe he has made, goodwill expressed as hostility to all that would unmake it. "The Son of God, Jesus Christ, was not Yes and No, but in him it is always Yes" (2 Cor. 1:19). Thus the Article says — and having said it, has said everything there is to say — that predestination to *life* is the everlasting purpose of God.

But, then, in the third place the Article identifies as the object of predestination "those whom he hath chosen in Christ out of mankind". Here the difference with the Westminster Confession is striking. Where the Calvinist document says that God *first* predestines "angels and men, particularly and unchangeably designed", and then fore-ordains Christ as the "means thereunto", the Article puts Christ at the heart of the eternal decree. (The Confession, too, speaks in §5 of "choosing in Christ"; but it annuls the force of this expression by the emphasis on particular predestination in §4 and the description of Christ as "means" in §6.) The Article does not teach a *particular* predestination of named individuals; there is simply the decree to save "those chosen in Christ". There will be a company of redeemed gathered around Christ the Representative: "All that the Father gives me will come to me" (Jn. 6:37). Who they will be is not specified before the foundations of the earth. God has predestined a community, but not its individual members. This point is underlined in the third paragraph, where we are instructed, as a matter of correctly reading Scripture, to understand the promises of God "generally", which is to say, generically, as addressed not to particular elect individuals but to the class of human-beings who will hear and obey God's word. That individuals arbitrarily refuse to hear is not to be explained by reference to divine decrees. (The Edwardian Articles said more about this refusal: an Article which bridged the gap between our numbers 16 and 17 stated that the blasphemy against the Holy Spirit was "when a man of malice and stubborness of mind, doth rail upon the truth of God's word manifestly perceived.")

In the classic doctrine, then, the individual and his destiny are rooted in eternity, while Christ and the community appear only in history to serve the outworking of the eternal decree. But in Cranmer's doctrine, as I have been presenting it, Christ and his community have their rooting in God's eternal decree, while the individual and his destiny appear only in history as the working out of that decree. It will be seen how the classic doctrine would force us in the direction of economic trinitarianism, and how the Calvinist organization of theology has the effect of leaving the doctrine of the Trinity up in the air. As rightly understood, however, the doctrine of predestination arises directly out of the doctrine of the Trinity and demonstrates that the history of salvation is the true expression of God's eternal trinitarian existence.

There remains one question which the Article does not broach. It asserts that God has chosen his community "out of mankind". How are we to reconcile this division within mankind, between the faithful and the unfaithful, with our insistence that God's word in creation is not Yes and No, but simply Yes? The answer emerges in the heart of Paul's discussion of Israel's election in Romans 9, where he explains that the "hardening" of Pharaoh had a purpose: "to make known (God's) might and make known the wealth of his glory on the vessels of mercy" (9:23). The dialectic of belief and unbelief within history, the refusal of the gospel by some and the rejection of unbelievers, serves, in God's providence, a revelatory purpose. It enables him to spread the knowledge of his goodness and saving deeds wider. The classic doctrine of predestination posits a self-justifying division of mankind into two camps; this division serves no purpose in redemption, but it simply given. But as the Bible explains Israel's election, it is a sign to the watching world that God is a mighty saviour, and therefore serves God's purpose that the world should come to believe. Even unbelief itself, when it comes into conflict with the elect people, serves this purpose. Israel's election was not oriented towards the exclusion of the Gentiles (however it may have been understood in a later, more defensive period) but towards their inclusion in a world that would glorify Israel's Lord. As is promised to the Elect One himself, the "servant" of Deutero-Isaiah: "It is too light a thing that you should be my servant to raise up the tribes of Jacob and to restore the preserved of Israel; I will give you as a light to the nations, that my salvation, may reach to the end of the earth" (Isa. 49:6).

How, then, shall we understand the phrase, "out of" mankind? First we must say, as the Article does, that we are chosen to enjoy that salvation which God has wrought *for* mankind in Christ. But then we must add that our election *out of* mankind, like that of Christ himself, is intended to serve mankind. We are to be carriers of the blessing which is for the rest of mankind as well as for us. He, the Chosen One, was chosen that we might be chosen "in him". We are chosen in him that others may be chosen in him through us. Election is like the effect of a magnet passing over iron filings: the magnet picks up some filings immediately, and then, through them, picks up others, which pick up others, and so on. Election is not election unless it works *through* us, as well as being enjoyed *by* us.

7

THE DISAPPEARANCE OF THE INVISIBLE CHURCH
(Article 19)

As we embark upon the second half of our document, we meet another of the Articles' strange silences. In discussing Article 17 we noticed that Cranmer failed — or deliberately omitted — to follow up his first statement about 'predestination to life' with a subsequent statement about 'foreordination to damnation', thus giving the Article a lopsided appearance. In Article 19 the same thing happens. It begins, "the visible church of Christ . . ." but never goes on to say anything about the invisible church. And once again it is helpful to make a contrast with the Westminster Confession, representing the Augustinian mainstream of Protestant thought. Chapter 25 of the Confession begins with a statement about "the catholic or universal Church, which is invisible", and then continues in §2 with a further statement about "the visible Church, which is also catholic or universal under the Gospel".

Why, in the first place, would one want to call the catholic church "invisible"? There are three possible justifications for this epithet. One is that there is a tension between an outward weakness and an inner strength in the church's life. Outwardly the church is powerless, ineffective, threatened with extinction; inwardly it is kept secure, protected in God's providence until Christ's glory is revealed on the last day. In Revelation 12:7ff. we read of how the dragon (Satan), cast down from heaven, made war upon the woman clothed in the sun with the moon beneath her feet, who is both Israel and the church.

The woman was given wings to fly away from the dragon to a place where she would be kept safe. So the dragon, in wrath, turned to make war upon "her children". Now, this warfare against the woman's children is clearly intended to mean the persecution of particular churches in John's own time; but the allegory tells us that while the children are persecuted, the mother is safe; that is, the empirical churches are threatened while the church itself, in its inmost reality, is kept secure. In this sense one might wish to speak of the invisible church — but not as some *other* church than the visible one: rather as the invisible reality which *underlies* the visible church, which we can know only by faith, yet in confidence because of the promises of God.

A second reason for calling the church invisible is that we must enter it by faith, and faith does not belong to the realm of appearances. The true believer can never be distinguished with certainty from the hypocrite. Thus Luther writes of the church as "a spiritual unity" which is "not a physical assembly but an assembly of hearts in one faith". There are two quite different ways, he says, of using the terms "church" and "Christendom". They can refer to the divinely-instituted "spiritual, internal Christendom" or to the man-made "physical, external Christendom". A third reason, which belongs with the classic doctrine of predestination, is that the church consists of the elect, who are unknown to us because their names and number, chosen by God in eternity, are in principle inaccessible. The visible church, contrasted with this invisible company, is the number of those who *profess* true religion. These two reasons both make a strong opposition (though on different grounds) between the real and the phenomenal, a contrast which goes much further than the paradox of strength in weakness.

But whichever reason or combination of reasons we find persuasive in leading us to speak of the catholic church as "invisible", we must be careful not to be seduced by the antithesis of visible and invisible into thinking that the only thing left to us in the realm of appearances is an *organization*. Luther's opposition of the two became at this point very misleading. He contrasted "an assembly in a house, or in a parish, a bishopric, an archbishopric or a papacy" on the one hand, with "the faith which makes true priests and Christians in the soul" on the other[1]. Luther was, of course, entirely justified in challenging the simple identification of the catholic church with an institution or organization of the church. But in allowing no middle term between the invisible and the organizational, he permitted the rhetoric of the

---

[1] *On the Papacy in Rome*, translated E.W. and R.C. Gritsch. *Luther's Works* Vol. 39, pp. 65-70.

outer-inner contrast to run away with him. For the catholic church, as catholic, is also visible — and that quite apart from any organization, whether house-church, parish, bishopric or papacy, which may express it. It is not merely something that is hidden, though in some aspects it may be hidden. It is an observable social reality which consists of all professing Christians, and as such belongs to the realm of appearances quite as definitely as its organizations do. Two music-lovers who correspond by letter about the sublimities of Mozart are hardly an invisible or internal fellowship merely because they have no organized musicological society at which to meet! And neither is the catholic church invisible or internal simply because it is not to be identified with the church institutions.

The reality of a pre-structural catholic society is acknowledged clearly in the next century by the Westminster Confession, which advances a trichotomous rather than a dichotomous analysis of the church, making not one, but two distinctions: between the catholic church which is invisible (§1) and the visible church which is also catholic, to which those belong who simply profess the Christian faith (§2); and then again between the visible catholic church and the "particular churches which are members thereof" (§4) — i.e. the church's organizations, which for prestbyterian polity are plural, though exactly the same distinction would have to be made if one believed in only one, universal organization.

This trichotomous analysis was not new, but was anticipated quite early in the sixteenth century, and anticipated, moreover, in documents which are central to the development of Anglican thought. Most strikingly, it is fully articulated in the Thirteen Articles of agreement between Anglicans and Lutherans in 1538, a document which Cranmer was happy to follow quite closely at other points in the composition of the Forty-Two Articles. In a truncated form (i.e., as a *dichotomous* analysis of the *visible* church), it appears in Jewel's *Apology* of 1561, the closest thing to an official doctrinal position-paper that emerged from the Elizabethan church during the first four years of the settlement. But Cranmer did not adopt it. In his own writings he was content with a dichotomous analysis of the church as a whole, in the style of Luther, distinguishing "the Holy Church . . . unknown to the world" and the "open known church" which is a "register or treasury to keep the books of God's Holy Will and Testament".[2] In his Articles he truncated this into a *unitary* account of the *visible* church, the account which we now have before us, left as it stood by Archbishop Parker whose mind was obviously less clear on

---

2 'On The Lord's Supper.' *Works of Archbishop Cranmer*, Parker Society, Vol. 1. p. 377.

the matter than that of Bishop Jewel. (The statement on the church in his own Eleven Articles of 1559, a provisional document which served to fill the gap until 1563, betrays something close to confusion.)

The disappearance of the invisible church from the Articles, then, carries with it as a corollary the total disappearance of the catholic church. For although Cranmer can from time to time in his writings acknowledge that the visible church is in fact universal, his dichotomous analysis does not allow him to disengage its visibility from the principles of its organization. He therefore plunges directly into a definition of the visible church in terms of its ministerial activity: "in the which the pure word of God is preached, and the sacraments be duly ministered". Contrast those verbs with the phraseology of the Thirteen Articles of 1538, which recognize the visible church "by the *profession* of the Gospel and *communion* in the sacraments". Contrast again the approach of Jewel, who can devote a whole paragraph to the doctrine of the visible church without mentioning the ministry, whether of preaching or sacrament: "We believe that there is one church of God and that the same is not shut up (as in times past among the Jews) into some one corner or kingdom, but that it is catholic and universal and dispersed throughout the whole world. So that there is now no nation which can truly complain that they be shut forth and may not be one of the church and people of God. And that this church is the kingdom, the body, and the spouse of Christ; and that Christ alone is the Prince of this kingdom; that Christ alone is the head of this body; and that Christ alone is the bridegroom of this spouse."[3]

In seeking to account for the silence of the Articles about the invisible church, and for their corresponding failure to speak distinctly about the visible catholic church, let us turn our attention back to Article 18, which summed up the section on salvation by saying that "Holy Scripture doth set out to us only the name of Jesus Christ, whereby men must be saved." This assertion may remind us of the famous mediaeval tag, *extra ecclesiam nulla salus*, "outside the church no salvation", a doctrine which goes back in one form or another to the patristic period and is especially associated with Cyprian of Carthage. It was usually understood in an uncompromisingly institutional sense, to mean that salvation depended on being in fellowship with the institutions of the catholic church, so that those who died in a schismatic fellowship, such as Novatianists or Donatists, would be damned. The reformers were perplexed by this doctrine. They could not accept its exclusivist claims for the church

[3] John Jewel, *An Apology of the Church of England* (Edited J.E. Booty), University Press of Virginia 1963, p.24.

institutions, especially when made on behalf of the late-mediaeval Roman see. On the other hand they did not wish to abandon the claim that salvation depended on belief in Christ. So they restated the exclusive claim, not as a claim for the church but as a claim for Christ. In this they believed (and with some justice) that they were reasserting the apostolic emphasis.

Thus a contributory reason for the silence of the Articles about the church might be that Cranmer, like other Reformers, wished to replace a great deal of what had been said about the church by Christology. He wished to exclude the church from the doctrine of salvation, in which it had so often played a usurper's role, and to focus attention upon Christ alone. There was a certain feeling abroad, which has often enough characterized Protestantism since, that talk about the church was not, strictly and in the most important sense, *theological* talk. "It is not ourselves we proclaim," said Saint Paul, "but Christ Jesus as Lord" (2 Cor. 4:5). If the gospel is not about the church, but about Christ, then so should theology, which is beholden to the gospel, make Christ and not the church the object of its attention. And that policy might have been very well if the Reformers had not been forced to tackle the serious constructive task of organizing their churches. As soon as they faced this task, all kinds of ecclesiological questions thrust themselves to the fore. On these issues, to do with the *institutions* of the church, the Reformers had plenty to say; the Articles themselves suggest the range and extent of their concerns. But between this practical institutional concern on the one hand and their understanding of the gospel on the other there was an unbridged hiatus, created by their reticence to speak about the church theologically. The ecclesiastical theory of the Reformation was tacked on as a large and overgrown appendix to an evangelical theology which had no real place for the church. This hiatus is what we now encounter at the beginning of this last major section of the Articles.

The hiatus is, perhaps, even more noticeable in the Edwardian Articles, where Cranmer actually did supply a bridge between Article 18 and this Article (his twentieth) on the visible church. The Article he placed there — part of which Parker incorporated into Article 7 on the Old Testament — spoke of the obligation of every man ("be he never so perfect a Christian") to keep the moral law taught in the Scriptures, and criticised antinomian extremists, who "do boast themselves continually of the spirit". The connexion, then, between the name of Jesus Christ whereby we must be saved and the ordered church institutions, is provided by the solitary Christian man living in obedience to the law of Christ — by that and nothing else, no community of believers, no redeemed humanity, no city of God. The implications of this theological hiatus have been serious, and have affected Protestantism to this day. Protestants have leaned towards an individualistic understanding of the gospel, proclaimed by arbitrary and schismatic institutions. The very tendency of Protestantism to break up into rival institutions has been fostered by the sense that the number and organization of these institutions does not matter.

The Church of England, as will appear more clearly, cannot be accused of ever having held such a view. Nevertheless, this lacuna in early Anglican thinking can only have encouraged it. For all its boasted "high-churchmanship", Anglicanism rested upon a formulary which opened the door to the arbitrary aspects of Protestant ecclesiology in a way that Calvinist documents, however radical their break with ecclesiastical tradition, did not.

There has to be a bridge between evangelical theology and ecclesiastical theory; that is, there has to be a theology of the church as such, which in turn will be the basis for the administrative tasks of church organization. That theology must not detract from the place of Christ at the centre of the gospel message. Yet to speak of the work of Christ it is necessary to speak of its result: a restored humanity, with Christ as its head, living in the light of God's presence. The catholic church is as much of that restored humanity as we have so far been given to see, a community in which the Holy Spirit dwells, expectantly anticipating the revealing of God's Kingdom. Anyone who believes in Christ in response to the apostles' testimony and has the Holy Spirit dwelling within him is *ipso facto* part of the catholic church. *Extra ecclesiam nulla salus,* though perilously open to misunderstanding, has its own validity when properly applied.

This is why speaking of the catholic church is a different thing from speaking of the institutional church which can determine its own limits, make conditions of recognized membership, count its adherents, and so on. The catholic church cannot do any of these things. It is simply created by the Holy Spirit's work in bringing members of the human race to believe in Christ. And yet this amorphous company needs to find institutional forms. If it is to serve as a sign of the coming Kingdom, then it must have a coherence and order which expresses the character of the Kingdom appropriately. A community which was evanescent and transitory could hardly be a sign of the eternal kingdom. A community which was confused and uncertain about its faith could hardly be a sign of the full clarity of God's presence. A community which lacked sufficient organization either to meet or to act together, for worship or for witness, could not represent the effective freedom of God's rule. In order to be what it is called to be, the catholic church must be embodied in institutional churches which, besides being "visible", do have some organizational definition.

We say "churches" — but should we not say "church"? Ought not the institutional embodiment of the catholic church to be *one*, as the catholic church itself is one, and as Jesus, its head, is one? Certainly it ought, and that is why ecumenism makes an unconditional demand upon all church institutions. It is not a question of creating a unity which does not now exist, but of giving appropriate institutional expression to the unity which the catholic church (which we declare in the creed is "one") already possesses — or rather, we may say, giving *more adequate* institutional expression, for even at the institutional level unity is not simply lacking. Ecumenism is one of the ways in which the institutions of the church must be shaped and re-shaped to express the truth of the church itself more adequately than they do. But, of course, not any form of institutional unity will be appropriate. It must be a kind of unity which corresponds to the unity which the Holy Spirit gives, a unity which can comfortably embrace the diversities of gifts, operations and services within the united confession that "Jesus is Lord". Unity of the wrong kind will fail, just as disunity fails, to make the church institutions an effective sign of the gospel.

There is an inescapable tension, we must confess, between our experience of the church in its catholic wholeness and the institutional churches which seek to give it expression. No institution is so supple and discriminating that it can correspond exactly to the truth of the church. Particularly is this so in our own age, when the institutional embodiments, shattered into a thousand pieces by successive theological crises (of which the Chalcedonian Christological formula was the earliest to leave a surviving schism, the ordination of women the most recent), do not even begin to comprehend the fullness of Christ's church at this point in history. But in every age it has been so, partly because of the disobedience of individual Christians who have been arrogant and disrespectful towards the institutions, partly because of the clumsiness of the institution and its failure to be sufficiently adaptable. And this tension may tempt us to move in one of two directions: either to think of the church in purely institutional terms, and forget the fact that the institutions are much less than the whole (the tendency traditionally associated with Roman theology, though by no means unique to it); or to abandon the institution altogether in favour of individualism and such ephemeral expressions and experiences of fellowship in the church as chance, rather than order, may bring our way.

Both temptations must be resisted. The tension must be maintained in our experience. And to maintain it we must recognize, on the one hand, that institutional churches *are* proper and authentic expressions of the catholic church, and, on the other, that: "as the Church of

Jerusalem, Alexandria and Antioch have erred; so also the Church of Rome hath erred". And, we may add, every "particular" church that has ever existed or does exist has erred. It is for this reason that we must remain humble about our institutions and resist the temptation to identify this or that one with the catholic church. The Church of Rome has not been mistaken in believing that there is a sense in which infallibility and inerrancy ought to be attributed to the catholic church; did not Jesus promise that the Holy Spirit would guide us into all truth? But it failed until recent times to acknowledge the equally certain truth that error must be attributed to all particular churches, including itself.[4] The churches we encounter as institutions are always lagging behind that reality of the catholic church in history, as God is bringing it constantly to existence.

So, then, we reckon with the church catholic as a reality in history; we reckon with the particular churches which give institutional embodiment to the church catholic and yet never fully measure up to it. Can we say any more about these particular churches? It is dangerous to try. For the attempt to characterize what a valid institutional expression of the church must be can all too easily assume the appearance of exclusiveness. Throughout the history of the church, doctrines of the "marks" of the church have been used as weapons with which one institutional body has tried to disqualify others from counting as churches at all. Thus the doctrine that the church must be "one, holy, catholic, apostolic" was used in the patristic period as a polemic doctrine, directed against schismatic bodies by Catholics. And the Reformation doctrine, first spelled out by the Confession of Augsburg (Art. 7), that "a church is a congregation of saints in which the Gospel is rightly preached and the sacraments rightly administered", was used to disqualify Anabaptist groups which abandoned the sacraments. The Anglican church has itself been guilty of devising exclusive criteria for churchliness, which have allowed it to discount bodies which did not meet its standards. The Lambeth Quadrilateral of 1888 stipulated, as a condition of intercommunion with any church body, that it must have the Bible, the Creeds, the Sacraments and — "the historic episcopate", a bullying and unfriendly gesture to the non-episcopal churches which history, and Anglican second thoughts, have happily overtaken.

Down this dangerous road of specifying the marks of an insti-

---

[4] For the Roman Catholic view in our own day, cf. the words of H. Fries & J. Finsterhölzl: "The history of the infallible Church . . . must be balanced by a realistic view of the *fallibilitas ecclesiae*." *The Concise 'Sacramentum Mundi'*, art. "Infallibility", p.717.

tutional church Cranmer undertook to travel, taking the two marks of Augsburg which remained normative for sixteenth-century Protestantism — "the pure word of God is preached, and the sacraments be duly ministered". We must regret, I think, that he took this road, and allowed any non-Christological title-deeds for the recognition of a church. It was a step towards giving the particular church, the institution, a kind of independence of the saving work of Christ, and also allowing it to usurp for itself the place of the catholic church. Nevertheless, all is not lost in this move, if we understand these marks not as *criteria* for any claim to be a church, but as *demands* that any church should seek to meet. There is a place for saying that the church *must* preach the Word of God faithfully and *must* administer the sacraments; provided that we mean that these things are a *primary responsibility*, the duty of any group of Christian believers who organize themselves for worship and witness. Thus, with respect to the sacraments, for example, we can address the non-sacramental churches not with a curt definitional *fiat*, declaring that they are simply *not* churches, but with a challenge to them to join us in common obedience to the command of Christ. If they are to organize themselves as Christian believers, should they not do it in the way that Christ laid down? Will their effectiveness as a witnessing and worshipping institution of the church not be enhanced by simple obedience at this point? Similarly we address those bodies who appear to us to have a defective Christian doctrine while yet confessing Jesus as the Christ, not with a definitional exclusion, but with a summons to the common task of giving more adequate expression and belief to that truth from which the church draws its life. The question is not whether they *are* "a church" — for if they confess Christ they cannot be anything else — but how much longer they will continue to be one unless they seek to organize their life and worship together in these basic ways.

To institutions which do meet these two demands, as well as those which do not, we are bound to address a challenge. We must constantly bring our institutions more closely into line with the reality of the catholic church, to which the holy Spirit is daily adding, and which he is building up around us.

8

AUTHORITY TO COMMAND
(Articles 32-39)

"The church hath power to decree rites or ceremonies, and authority in controversies of faith." So begins Article 20, with an echo from the Confession of Würtemberg, added, if the conjecture be true, by Elizabeth herself. Power and authority are the principle subjects of the remaining twenty Articles; "power" is understood in the sense of an authority to make arbitrary decisions on matters inessential to the integrity of Christian faith, "authority" in the sense of a capacity to teach and expound the Christian faith in a way which makes its demands in any new situation apparent. Most of the remaining Articles (though not all of them) are concerned with the exercise of these two kinds of authority within the church. Cranmer, whose outline still controls the structure of the Elizabethan Articles even though they make many more revisions to this last section than they have hitherto, treats first of the teaching authority of the church, later of its government — and from the point of view of logical sequence this is obviously the better way, giving the whole document the character of a descent from the most essential realities to the most inessential: God, Christ, revelation, salvation, proclamation and administration. But this approach depends on the idea of authority being immediately comprehensible, which to the modern reader it is not. So I shall beg the indulgence of an extensive re-ordering of the material, simply for ease of exposition, taking matters in the sequence that the first sentence of Article 20 suggests.

"Authority" means that which initiates, but specifically it refers to that which initiates free thought and action. The initiator of a mechanical chain of events is not an "authority" but a "cause". Authority is exercised over those who act for themselves. Yet there may be different kinds of authority, and eliciting different kinds of activity. Some authority evokes thought, some deed. There is authority which gives rise to spontaneous action, and authority which gives rise to deliberated action. Sometimes the response is reluctant and grudging, sometimes unreserved and glad. A full account of the idea would take us far beyond the scope of the Articles, which are interested in two kinds of authority only, as exercised in two different social contexts. They are interested in the authority of *true speech*, which persuades minds and instils convictions; and they are interested in the authority of *legitimate command*, which orders and directs the conduct of social life. Broadly speaking, they maintain the position that the church, as "the witness and a keeper of Holy Writ", exercises the former authority in society, and the monarch the latter.

The question of how these two authorities relate to each other has been one of the perennial questions of Western political thought, since (we may say) Socrates was executed. Merely to distinguish them, of course, gets us no further than posing the problem: not all rulers command with the authority of wisdom, not all wise men speak with the authority of rulers. This generates a constant struggle. Those who hold legitimate political authority are anxious to secure their position against the erosion of the confidence in which men hold them — for the belief that rulers are wrong can result in the collapse of their authority to command. Those, on the other hand, who have some wisdom may find it intolerable to live within the constraints imposed by the rule of the foolish. Thus from both sides arise aspirations to unite the two authorities in one. Plato speculated about a polity in which the philosophers would rule, Marx about the state which was authenticated by science.

Christian political thought must begin from the conviction that the two authorities both have their source in God — for "there is no authority but from God" (Rom. 13:1). Theologians (following Thomas) have sometimes developed this idea by saying that in God reason and will are not distinct; so that the ultimate truth (which claims the reason) and the ultimate command (which claims the will) are not different realities, but one reality. And in Jesus the unity of truth and command is in some measure apparent. Saint Mark tells us how the crowds, amazed at his teaching and miracles, cried: "What is this? A new teaching, with authority! He even commands the unclean spirits and they obey him!" (1:27) and Saint John how, at the self-declaring word "I am he", the soldiers who came to arrest him stepped backwards and stumbled to the ground (18:6). Yet precisely because such a union of authorities belongs to the being of God himself and to his Kingdom in Christ, Christian thought (in the West, at least) has been suspicious of attempts to reunite them in earthly political systems. In the social orders which prevail until the coming of Christ, the authority of truth and the authority of command had better be kept explicitly distinct, since in practice any attempt to embody the whole truth in a political order must lead to disillusionment. For this reason Western Christian thought has tended to favour the development of a "liberal" theory, which separates the authorities, rather than of an ideological totalitarianism.

The Tudors are not (and with good reason) usually held up as models of a liberal political order; nevertheless, we must be struck by the emphasis which their theologians placed on the distinction of the two authorities. They may have been autocratic, but they were not totalitarian. It is not only Parker's explicit statement in Article 37 to which we can refer: "we give not to our princes the ministering either of God's word, or of sacraments," important as that is. Once again we find in the order of the Articles a strong indication, the more reliable because the less explicit, of how Cranmer and his successors viewed the issues at large. They present five Articles relating to the teaching authority of the church (20-24), follow them with a treatment of the sacraments in seven Articles (25-31 in the 1571 version; in 1563 there were six, in 1553 five), five Articles on diverse points of church order (32-36); and only then come to "the civil magistrates" and matters relating to social order (37-39). The order corresponds (with one interesting difference to which we shall return) to that adopted in Calvin's *Institutes*, where it is explicitly based on the theory of "a twofold government in man".

But it is a matter of some difficulty for the modern reader to grasp that this division of authorities does *not* imply the distinction of what we call "church and state". Those words, though they are cheerfully set by some commentators at the head of these Articles, must be repudiated as utterly misleading. The very word "state", of course, is used ambiguously by moderns with two distinct meanings: it sometimes represents the Greek *politeia* and the Latin *respublica*, which mean the politically organized community as a whole; but it is also, and more commonly, used to mean the distinctly political structures *within* the community, as opposed to all other aspects of the community's life, and it is in this sense that we make our contrast, not only between the state and the individual, but between the state and the church, the state and the universities, the state and business etc., etc. Now, this modern conception of the state as a department of society was not known to the Tudors and begins to make its appearance (in English thought at least) only in the seventeenth century. The Tudors did not conceive of society as divided (in Althusian fashion) into self-governing departments, each with its own proper area of concern. Thus they did not draw what might seem to us to be the obvious conclusion from the principle of twofold authority: that the monarch should not interfere with the affairs of the church, and that the church should not interfere with the affairs of state. The American revisers of the Articles in 1801 could not, in their own political circumstances, avoid redrafting Article 37 in this sense, distinguishing the power of the civil magistrate "in all things temporal" from authority "in things purely spiritual". The conception of distinct temporal and spiritual spheres of authority came as naturally to them as it does to us; but the Tudors could never have formulated their theory in such terms. For them the matter was more complex (and rightly so). The life of the church, too, fell under the jurisdiction of the monarch, insofar as the church, too, needed the direction and government of one who had the authority to command. Even the international activities of the church (as the first sentence of Article 21 claims) fell under the collective authority of "princes". The authority of the ruler extended over the whole of society "whether . . . ecclesiastical or civil". But, then, so did the authority of God's word extend over the whole of society. We do not often find the Tudor theologians drawing this corollary explicitly, but it is clearly assumed, not least in the permissive clauses of Articles 37 and 39. "It is lawful for Christian men, at the commandment of the magistrate, to wear weapons . . ." What law is this which permits the magistrate so to command but the law of God? "Christian religion doth not prohibit but that a man may swear when the magistrate requireth, in a cause of faith and charity . . ." What law does not prohibit its subjects from obeying the civil magistrate, "so it be done according to the prophet's teaching, in justice, judgement, and truth", a condition which certainly limits the magistrate's requirement as surely as the subject's compliance with it? The "godly prince", to whom the prerogative of command is given, is one who is obliged above all to the authority of God's word. In the next century, again, this aspect of things drops out of sight, and seventeenth-century Anglicanism is marked by the growth of an absolutist theory of monarchical authority, reflecting, like the negative of a photograph, the absolutist conceptions of popular sovereignty which were steadily gaining ground throughout Europe.

Society, then, is one society, and the monarch's writ runs everywhere within it, though always (and again, in every aspect of social life) subject to the critical authority of the word of God, which the monarch himself does not have the authority to expound or

preach. The suffrages of Cranmer's Litany give us a perfect outline of
how society, as the Tudors saw it, was organized. Initially, there is a
suffrage for the church (under which all society is included), that God
will rule and govern it in the right way; then for the king, that God
may rule *his* heart 'in thy faith, fear, and love', and give him victory
over all his enemies; then for the clergy, that 'both by their preaching
and living' the word of God may be unambiguously proclaimed; after
which we pray for the king's civil counsellors, for the magistrates, and
for 'all thy people', i.e. of England, and finally for 'all nations'. Having
thus sketched the structure of society in a few brush-strokes, we pray
for it as a whole, treating it entirely seriously as a Christian society in
every respect: "that it may please thee to give us an heart to love and
dread thee, and diligently to live after thy commandments," "to hear
meekly thy word" and "to bring forth the fruits of the Spirit"; that
God will bring into the way of truth all such as have erred, comfort
the weak-hearted, and beat down Satan under our feet. We will not
grasp the Tudor conception of society unless we appreciate that these
prayers are offered, and in these terms, not for a congregation of
believers gathered out of society, but for the Lords of the council in
parliament, for the magistrates on the bench and for the royal armies
in combat. The suffrages which then follow, to our eyes of a more
obviously secular kind, thus run on quite naturally, and there is
equally no sense of hiatus when they are rounded up with a prayer for
"true repentance", forgiveness, and the grace of the Holy Spirit "to
amend our lives according to thy holy word". When we say that
Litany today, we are forced mentally to change the reference of the
first person plural pronoun: "we" are now the gathered congregation
of faithful believers obligated to the word of God, now the whole
society of mankind in its political organization, beset with its secular
affairs. Not so the Tudor Christians who first prayed in these words.
words.

What are we to make of this account of authority, so sharply
different from anything that comes naturally to us who are separated
from it by the revolutions in political thought which swept across
Europe in the seventeenth and eighteenth centuries, and so sharply
different again from anything of which the New Testament church
could have conceived? We must beware, in the first place, of assuming
that because the unity of church and society, assumed as a matter of
course by the Tudors, is plainly not a view that can claim authority
from apostolic times, therefore our own modern form of liberalism,
with its departmental categorizations of secular and sacred, is any
closer to the apostolic tradition. Although it is true that we, like the
New Testament itself, conceive, perforce, of the church as a body of
believers gathered *out* of society, and the Tudors did not; it is

doubtful whether our attempts to demarcate, and so legitimize, the lines of separation between church and society by means of the secular-sacred distinction do not do more violence to the wide-ranging claims of the apostolic gospel than did the mediaeval and Reformation attempts to abolish the line of separation entirely. The apostolic view of society saw it as distinct from the church, certainly; yet the two were always in competition for the same territory of human loyalties, laying claim to the whole of life for their respective goods. That they conceded the legitimacy of political and judicial functions as a "secular" provision (that is, for the present *saeculum* or "age") is perfectly true. Yet that concession stops short of the modern demarcation of a whole *secular sphere of life*, where the word of God does not rule as of right but finds access only indirectly, shaping the conscience of certain participants, who are also (but secretly) participants in the sacred sphere and so, in a manner of speaking, undercover agents for God. At least this much must be said for the conception of the Reformers: they laid a better foundation in principle for asserting the claims of God's word over all our social life. And if, from the advantage of our comfortable concordat with the political order, we are tempted to adopt a superior tone with them, decrying the craven manner of their dealings with princes and potentates, then we ought to recall that theirs was an enagagement in real earnest, the end of which was sometimes martyrdom. They knew what it could mean to uphold God's word before kings, and sometimes they upheld it in ways that drew them as close as could be desired to the suffering martyrs of the apostolic age.

Yet it is right to say that the Reformers' conception of the place of princes in the society of the faithful followed no model in the New Testament. Political theory is always interwoven with history, and their political theory, like that of the middle ages, had to come to grips with a historical reality unknown to the apostolic age, the conversion of society as a whole to Christian allegiance. The changes that they made to the mediaeval conception were forced upon them by their negative reevaluation of the papacy, which had played the (increasingly controversial) double role of an international political force and a voice bearing witness to Christian truth. The English way of resolving the vacuum in political theory created by the rejection of papal claims was to draw together all explicitly political authority into the hands of the king. As we know, this solution was not long-lived, and proved less fruitful in terms of shaping the political life of the modern age than the alternative solutions reached within Calvinist societies, especially in Switzerland and the Netherlands. However, it was a genuine attempt to find an order of Christian authenticity in a situation for which the New Testament gave no guidance. In search of models, the Reformers turned elsewhere to discover what had "been given always to all godly princes in Holy Scriptures by God himself", and found guidance from the patterns of authority established in the Davidic monarchy in ancient Israel.

Now, we are immediately inclined to regard this as a false step, because of the unique meaning of the monarchy in Judah as an expression of the covenant of election between God and his chosen people. The Davidic king is not a paradigm of all monarchs, but an agent of divine revelation. Israel and Judah were, in the proper sense of the word, conceived in totalitarian terms; that is to say, the authority of divine word and the authority to command were not to be separated. "I will tell of the decree of the Lord," says the king (Ps.2:7). "He said to me: 'You are my son, today I have begotten you.' " And against that divine word nothing can stand. This is why the failure of the Davidic kings to fulfil their responsibilities adequately, and the consequent rejection of the monarchy, meant, in the view of the prophets, nothing less than the end of the elect nation as such. And this prophetic judgment has shaped not only the Christian understanding of Jesus, but also the political theory which comports with it. For the restoration of a king in whom the two authorities are united cannot be conceived apart from the coming of God's self-revealing rule, that is to say in the universal reign of the Messiah, who is also the "shoot from the stump of Jesse" (Isa. 11:1). To justify the powers of Edward VI on the grounds of what God permitted to Josiah, as Cranmer did in his Coronation Speech, is to make a mistake exactly analogous to expounding the sacrificial role of the Christian priesthood on the basis of what was given to Levi. It is to miss the eschatological meaning of these institutions, and to expose oneself to the temptation of hallowing structures of this age with authority which belongs only to the glorified Messiah.

That neither Parker nor his Lutheran exemplars were unaware of the difficulties surrounding an appeal to the "godly princes" of Scripture we may take for granted. Parker himself, in the same Article 37, has insisted upon the separation of the teaching and ruling authorities. What he really needed to find in Scripture was some model of monarchy (or simple principality) which displayed the *natural* features of government (i.e. apart from the Davidic covenant) in their best light; but the Old Testament is unhappily lacking in such models. The nearest one could find would be the Persian monarchs who ruled the Holy Land at the time of Ezra and Nehemiah. But was Parker mistaken in thinking that princely government could also be viewed as a natural institution of human life, and that certain things could be said, even on the basis of the Davidic example and the royal psalms, about what monarchy — any monarchy — ought to be and do? If we say so, then the usefulness of the Old Testament for our understanding of social justice is virtually annulled at one stroke. When the prophets rebuke the kings about their failures to give judgment for the poor, or when the king solemnly swears to walk with integrity of heart within his house, we can hardly think that these are only religious matters, uniquely dependent on the Messianic role of David's son. We immediately suppose that all rulers are meant to hear and imitate. There is, then, in the Davidic monarchy also a model of what kings as such should rightly be. But that this model authorizes the Tudors in placing the government of the church directly in royal hands: that, we must say, is to stretch the argument further than it will rightly go.

We must, however, admire the Tudor settlement for having grasped something of importance very firmly. It bequeathed to subsequent generations of the Church of England — and to modern Anglicans throughout the world — a sharp sense of the distinction between those matters of church order which embodied fundamental theological principle and those matters which could be thought of as variable from one condition of society to another. Precisely because the monarch had discretion to command in questions of the latter sort, the distinction had to be made, and made clearly. Not all subsequent generations of Anglicans have grasped it as it ought to have been grasped; had they done so, perhaps, the Restoration of 1660 would have been an altogether more tolerant and less tyrannical affair. Nevertheless, the memory that there *is* a distinction has remained with us and come to our aid at crucial moments of difficulty, giving the Anglican church order that characteristic manoeuverability within bounds of principle which is the delight of some and the despair of others. Most recently this memory has served us by preserving our unity in the difficult debate over the ordination of women as priests. We remarked earlier on a difference between the order of subjects followed in the Articles and the order of the fourth book of Calvin's 1559 Institutes. It is this: where Calvin treats first of the church, second of the sacraments and third of civil government, the Anglican Articles have removed certain matters concerning the *discretionary* order of the church, distinguishing them from the *essential* order of the church, and have dealt with them in a separate section (Articles 32-36) placed just before the exposition of the powers of civil government. And as requirements of our own exposition have compelled us to reverse the order followed by the Articles, and approach the whole question of authority through the back door, we will proceed in keeping with this looking-glass logic and complete our account of the authority-to-command with a more detailed consideration of this discretionary church-order.

In Article 34 Parker writes: "Every particular or national church, hath authority to ordain, change and abolish ceremonies or rites of the church ordained only by man's authority, so that all things be done to edifying." There is, in other words, an authority posited simply by the church's self-organization in "particular churches". The "particular", that is, the institutional church, which the Anglican Reformers thought should be organized coextensively with political units as the "national church" (i.e. the church of the nation, *not* "state-church") needs to be able to make decisions, to make rules for conduct and organization, to define itself in terms of its membership and the conditions of membership. In order to be an effective body witnessing in the world, the national church must structure itself as an institution, which means it must have its own pattern of government. That government would not have to be vested in the king; it might be vested in bishops, synods, or congregations; but still it must be there. Indeed, if it were not organized nationally but internationally, it would still need such government, and the same would apply if it were organized on a purely civic or congregational basis. But this is "authority" in quite a different sense from the teaching authority derived from Christ and the Apostles. This is an institutional or political authority arising *within* the church, as opposed to a defining and determining authority of truth *over* the church.

Article 33, "of excommunicate persons", illustrates the need for such an institutional authority to impose discipline on church members. No one could have known better than the Reformers what a dangerous weapon excommunication could be when used unwisely or without proper obedience to the gospel. Many of the pioneers of the Reformation were excommunicated, and from one point of view nothing would have been more attractive than to attempt (what has now become the rule in all but the Roman and the smaller Protestant communities) the complete abolition of excommunication. Yet the Reformers knew that the church-as-institution could not dispense with means of defining itself. If the particular church was to be effective as an expression of the *church*, and not as something else, it had to have terms of membership. It had to ensure that it would continue to proclaim the Christian gospel and maintain a Christian moral witness. In New Testament times it appears that excommunication was exercised, and was justified by reference to a command of Christ himself. The solution, as the Reformers saw it, was not to abolish the "open denunciation of the church", but to establish the church more thoroughly on gospel principles, so that only those who really denied the Word of God, disobeyed the command of God or foreswore faith in Christ, would become the object of this unfavourable attention. And we should not let it go entirely without saying that any discipline that pretends to defend the gospel must be reversible: open denunciation must always envisage open reconciliation, otherwise it ceases to offer any kind of defence to the *Christian* gospel or the *Christian* church.

The opening words of Article 34, "It is not necessary that traditions and ceremonies be in all places one, or utterly like", define the Reformers' attitude to the church's institutional authority. It is an attitude which has two faces to it, attacking Rome on the one hand and certain Protestants on the other.

Firstly, in opposition to Rome, the Reformers maintain that the unity of the universal church, standing under the authority of the Lord and the apostles, does not require institutional expression by a single, uniform institutional structure. Unity in the gospel could be sustained, the Reformers believed, alongside institutional plurality. As they say in Article 37: "The bishop of Rome hath no jurisdiction in this realm of England." The Pope, the father of the church, has become "the bishop of Rome", with authority over one "particular" church among many. There is no need for an institutional focus of unity to link the various particular churches which express the universal reality of the catholic church. The classic mediaeval identification of the authority of the apostles with the authority of the pope was a mistake. It confused two quite distinct kinds of authority, and led to a totalitarian regime in which legitimate varieties of administration, perfectly compatible with unity in the apostolic testimony, were suppressed.

Two examples of this are given: one is in Article 36, which defends the right of the Church of England to revise the ordinal and the ceremonies attaching to it, and (by implication) denies that the ministry is dependent for its validity either upon historical continuity with the mediaeval tradition of orders or upon the recognition of the pope. The other example is in Article 32, which is, however, more than an example, and takes the definition of the church's governing authority further. The tradition which grew up in the early Middle Ages under the influence of monasticism, that the clergy should be unmarried, was imposed by the papacy upon the whole Western church during the great reforms of the eleventh century. The Reformers objected to the idea that the pope could impose this requirement. It is not a matter on which the Scripture gives any command, and so must at least be a matter for judgment by particular churches "according to the diversities of countries, times, and men's manners". There need be no *universal* requirement of celibacy among the clergy, because there is no universal governing authority within the church. But they state the matter more strongly than this, and suggest that no church may properly make this requirement anyway, because Scripture presents the question of marriage and singleness as one of *individual* vocation, on which, consequently, only the individual believer may decide. The question of married priests, then, defines a boundary beyond which no governing authority within the church may go — a right of the believer to private discretion. We should pause, in passing, to note the momentary appearance of an idea which, if some polemical accounts of the Reformation are to be believed, dominated it: the believer's private judgment. It is, on the whole, typical of Tudor Anglicanism that it is asserted only this once in the Articles (and is, indeed, given a sharp rebuff in Article 34!). The idea begins to play a large part in Anglican thought in the next century when the moralists, inspired, ironically enough, by Counter-Reformation examples, begin to discuss at length the individual's duties of conscience. In truth the whole question is a seventeenth-century one. In the Tudor period we find the believer's discretion defended only in relation to classic vocational choices: here, the decision to marry; in the Ordinal, the decision about calling to the sacred ministry.

How are we to assess the stance that the Reformers adopt in opposition to the papal claims for a united institutional structure? I think we must say that it is true, and yet not the whole truth. It is true that there is a unity within the catholic church, arising from its acknowledgement of Christ as Lord and its obedience to the apostolic testimony to Christ, that cannot be shaken even by institutional conflict, let alone by simple plurality. The twentieth century has rediscovered the fact, very much to its joy, that where there is common confession of Christ there is unity in him, whatever the denominational barriers or institutional oppositions. The ecumenical movement came of age when it realized that Christian unity was something to be celebrated, not merely to be sought after. It is true, also, that the failure to distinguish the authority of Christ and the apostles from the governing authority of the pope has continually tempted the Roman church in a totalitarian direction, and that this is still a problem for ecumenical relations despite the major new emphasis on "local churches" that has marked Roman thought in the past quarter-century.

Nevertheless, Scripture tells us not merely that we *have* unity in Christ, "One Lord, one faith, one baptism" (Eph.4:5), but that we must "guard the unity of the Spirit in the bond of peace" (4:3). Unity is a task as well as a gift. And in fulfilling that task Christians have found that institutional disaccord has been a great hindrance. Even if the Reformers' hopes had been fulfilled, and each political entity had come to have its own independent national church institution, distinct in administration but united with the others in faith, communication between churches might have been difficult. But their vision proved abortive. Roman tenacity on the one hand and dissenting tenacity on the other forced the government of England to concede, within little more than a century, a *de facto* pluralism within its territories. The sectarian situation had come into being, with all its concomitant rivalry, recrimination and bitterness. What remained of the national-church concept was further dissipated in the age of colonialism; and today, though the idea has some shadowy surviving validity in England, it can have no significance for the other churches of the worldwide Anglican communion, almost all of which are minority churches. It is hard to see how the pursuit of unity in the Spirit can proceed without seeking some measure of institutional reunion, even if it were only to modify practices which have been created by past attitudes of hostility and suspicion. Institutions are not totally indifferent; they help or they hinder the pursuit of unity in the Spirit. Institutional unity is therefore a reasonable and necessary goal of Christian endeavour, provided that it is not seen as the be-all and end-all of Christian unity, and provided that it safeguards the diversity and local integrity which is also the Spirit's gift.

The second face of the Reformers' attitude is turned towards the strand of Protestant opinion which was in fact present throughout the English Reformation, associated with Lollardry, but which gained new force and respectability after the Elizabethan settlement, which believed that the English Reformation was failing to establish a truly scriptural order. Against this view the Articles maintain that there is legitimate scope for variety in the dispositions made by different institutional churches 'according to the diversities of countries, times, and men's manners'. Unity in the gospel does not mean uniformity in all the decisions that the churches have to make. There are matters to be decided which, from the point of view of loyalty to Scripture, are indifferent. Not, of course, that there is nothing to choose one way or the other in all these matters. There may be right and wrong, wise and foolish decisions; theological arguments may be advanced, and positions defended. But the question of loyalty to Scripture does not decide them. In these matters the institutional church has a right, the Reformers believed, to expect its members to abide loyally by the decisions it makes, even if they wish the decisions had been made differently.

There was a particular issue which gave point to this demand, which Parker made the subject of a new Article (36) replacing Cranmer's more general Article endorsing the Book of Common Prayer. It was the sore grief of certain sections of the Elizabethan church that their national church, unlike the Reformed churches of Switzerland, had retained the episcopate. They could object, quite correctly, that the terms which designated presbyters and bishops in the New Testament were not differentiated but used interchangeably.

They objected also, with rather less clear success, that presbyter-bishops were always in groups, never single. Obedience to the scriptural model, they maintained, forbade the retention of the monarchical bishop. In the face of this the Church of England maintained its freedom to retain the monarchical episcopate if it saw fit. "It is evident unto all men, diligently reading Holy Scripture and ancient authors, that from the apostles' time, there have been these orders of ministers in Christ's church; bishops, priests and deacons . . . And therefore to the intent these orders may be continued, and reverently used and esteemed in the Church of England . . ." So Cranmer had written in the preface to his ordinal. Attention has focused upon the historical uncertainty of the assertion made in the first sentence of this preface, that the creation of monarchical bishops dates back to apostolic age, an assertion which depends on how the roles of Timothy and Titus should be interpreted. More interesting is the fact that, whether or not Cranmer thought that the three-tier ministry could be found in Scripture, he defended its retention on the grounds of tradition. He made no attempt to show that it is *required* in a scriptural order. Thus the retention of this order of ministry belongs within the sphere of legitimate freedom exercised by the church in its context. And so it was defended in the Tudor ages, even by such apologists as Richard Hooker who stressed its apostolic origin and the guidance of the Holy Spirit very strongly. The role of bishops was "positive, and consequently not absolutely necessary, but of a changeable nature because there is no divine voice which in express words forbiddeth it to be changed."[1]

Of this attitude, too, we may say that it is true, but not the whole truth. It is certainly true that not everything that was done by the New Testament church was meant as a universal principle of the church's existence. It is easy to agree that all churches are bound to baptize and celebrate the Lord's Supper (though we should note dissenters even to this opinion), and it is easy to agree that the apostles' action in Samaria does not resolve the question of whether there should or should not be a rite of confirmation. But how does one assess such an issue as the ordination of women as priests? Does Scripture say anything about it? Not directly, but there are instructions given by Saint Paul on the conduct of women in the churches which are hardly encouraging. Is Saint Paul, then, simply using his liberty in his circumstances as we may in ours? The difficulty here is that it is hard either for us or for Saint Paul to use our liberty either way without presuming on answers to theological questions on which Scripture does have something to say — the theology of sexuality in particular.

[1] *Laws of Ecclesiastical Polity* VII.5.8.

This seems to be an issue which it is hard to classify neatly into either one of the categories offered us by the Article, either as "tradition and ceremony" or as "God's word". It is a theological issue, closely but not immediately touched by Scripture. And perhaps every important issue of church government is like this notorious one of our own time. Yet, even if it is so, we are not bound to think that the distinction was, after all, of no use. The point of a good theory is not to save us the task of thinking, but to organize our thoughts fruitfully. The best distinctions can be the most difficult to apply, but are valuable because they formulate the most important questions that have to be answered. What is the complementarity of male and female? How and why should it be respected in an order of service and worship? What might the masculine and the feminine principles look like if they were embodied in complementary patterns of church ministry? And so on.

Certainly, in the matter of episcopacy it turned out that the measured defence of episcopacy as an institution reformable in principle but to be retained in practice, was not easy to sustain. In the seventeenth century its defenders were less inclined to measure the terms of their defence, just as its opponents were less measured in their opposition. In the confrontation of positions shaped by the institutional absolutisms of the age, something precious and central to the moderation of Anglican government was lost sight of. Fortunately, despite the terrible damage done by the events of Commonwealth and Restoration, it was not lost sight of for ever.

9

AUTHORITY TO CONVINCE
(Articles 20—24)

At a key point in the narrative of the three synoptic gospels Saint Peter declares, "You are the Christ, the Son of the living God". To this Jesus replies, according to St. Matthew's Gospel (16:18), "On this rock I will build my church." That first confession of faith in Christ, made by an eyewitness, becomes the touchstone for what it is, and is not, the Church of Jesus Christ. When that testimony was given the Church became possible. Others could identify themselves with it and echo Peter's words, making them their own. The church exists wherever men stand in solidarity with Peter in his profession of faith, and utter it with him. That is why we said at the end of Chapter 7 that we had no right to deny the name "church" where we found Jesus acknowledged as God's Messiah.

To this, however, we must add two important observations. In the first place, the confession of faith in Jesus which the church makes its own still remains *Saint Peter's* confession, the confession of the apostolic generation. It is not as though it had somehow been taken over from them, so that it was now entirely ours and no longer theirs. When the church of the twentieth century confesses Jesus as God's Messiah, it does so *with* Peter and *with* his apostolic contemporaries. It may appropriate Peter's words, but cannot expropriate them. It cannot pretend that this confession is something that it has invented for itself, a discovery of faith that is entirely its own. Nor can it pretend that it makes this confession on the authority of the church of the *nineteenth* century, its immediate predecessor. It is, of course, true that one generation tells another, but that does not mean that each generation looks for its authority to the faith of the one before it. The authority for the faith of every generation is the eyewitness testimony of the first generation, which, as eyewitness, is in a unique position. It is not just the first in the sense that there happens to be no generation before it. It is the foundation of the church, and the church can no more cut itself free from dependence upon it than a building can float free of its foundations. The church is "built upon the foundation of the apostles and prophets, Christ Jesus being the chief cornerstone" (Eph.2:20). Thus in being the Church, in making Peter's confession with him, the church of each generation is necessarily "apostolic", and cannot will to be otherwise without willing itself outside of Christ altogether.

In the second place, Saint Peter's confession stands as part of a much more extensive confession, partly Peter's own and partly that of his associates of the apostolic generation, which is the expansion and interpretation of that decisive and central confession that he made. I mean, of course, the New Testament as a whole. The New Testament is the totality of what this eyewitness generation was given to tell us about God's work in Jesus, just as Peter's famous sentence is the centre of it. We should interpret the whole in the light of the centre, and the centre in the light of the whole. It is the meaning of "heresy" that we can take the confession out of its proper interpretative context and hold to it as a form of words while refusing assent to the apostolic witness as a whole. There were those in the apostolic age, for example, who thought that they could make their peace with the confession without accepting that Jesus was the Christ "come in the *flesh*" (1 Jn. 4:2). Thus the place of heretics in the Church has always been ambiguous and uncertain. They have not stood wholly with the apostolic faith, nor wholly apart from it. There is an irresolution in their position, which must, in the end, settle itself one way or the other. The church, on the other hand, which has its existence by standing with Peter in his confession of faith, must be instructed from first to last by the New Testament.

The history of the church, then, is the social history of the conviction which Peter's confession has inspired. The authority of the church in its proclamation of the gospel is the authority of that God-given testimony. There is no other authority in teaching than the simple authority of the truth itself — or, perhaps, we should say, such other forms of authority as there may be are extrinsic to the task of teaching, and so, in the last analysis, irrelevant. Only the authority of the truth can convince. So when the Elizabethan Articles, following the Würtemberg Confession, declare that the church has "authority in controversies of faith", they mean nothing else than that the church, built upon the confession of Jesus as the Christ, has in that very confession the necessary source of illumination, and must not be afraid to call upon it.

This claim to teaching authority follows directly upon the last sentence of Article 19, where it is said that every particular church is liable to err. We must, therefore, read the claim carefully, neither exaggerating nor minimizing what it implies. It does not imply that, given a continuity of structural identity, the teaching offices of the church will never teach anything contrary to the truth. No doubt the Reformers believed that God would protect the church against falling wholly into error. But what may properly be said about the catholic church as a whole in this regard is by no means necessarily true of any institutional embodiment of it. There are religious bodies in existence which began their lives as Christian "churches", but which have ceased to be such because of a simple lack of resolution to stand firmly under the instruction of the New Testament. The Reformers were afraid that in their day the great church of Rome was inclined to travel dangerously far along that road. In no way, then, can they be understood to attribute infallibility to any particular teaching office. Yet at the same time they clearly do speak of an "authority" which belongs, not merely to the occasional prophet whom the Spirit may raise up, but to the institutional church. It has seemed to many that this was an attempt to find middle ground where no middle ground was. How can we understand it?

It is a most common mistake of modern absolutist political theory to suppose that a bearer of "authority" must in principle be above challenge and beyond confirmation. This is true neither of political nor of didactic authority. It is a more understandable mistake in the case of political authority, since it can point to a certain measure of arbitrariness which is inseparable from the exercise of command; but authority in teaching has nothing whatever to do with arbitrariness, and we would better understand political authority, too, if we ceased to think of arbitrariness as the normal case. The effective exercise of authority appeals to the confirmation of objective reality; and the more successfully it brings reality to light, the more effective it is as an exercise of authority. The authoritative command it the one which, even as it is uttered, strikes people as right. Not that they themselves would have been able to see it, or act in that way *apart* from the command; rather, the command itself brings the right course to light and enables people to see what should be done. Similarly — and more obviously — the authoritative teacher is the one whose teaching can illuminate, and so verify itself by, the realities of which it speaks. To take a formal example: someone who expounds a text, let us say a work of Plato, will be authoritative if, and only if, those who read Plato find that the text is illuminated and clarified by what the expositor says. He is authoritative precisely because Plato's text confirms his exposition. I do not mean that if on many previous occasions he has proved able to illuminate Plato's text, then on a subsequent occasion, where what he says is not self-evidently borne out by the text, we will nevertheless believe him. That may well be the case, and is an *implication* of his having authority; but it is not the *paradigm case* of authority. Authority is not a matter of being believed when you do not seem to be right. Nor is it being believed when you say what everybody knew anyhow. The paradigm case of authority is *making the truth appear* by your words; so that as you speak, people can see that you are right, and can see it by virtue of the evident truth which your words have illuminated.

When we attribute authority not just to a given utterance but to the person who has made it, we do so partly aposteriori, on the basis of our past experience of his authoritative words, and partly apriori, in view of what it is reasonable to expect of him in the light of his studies. When we attribute it to an institution or an office the same is true: of a journal or a society, for example, we may say that it has authority to speak on a subject when its words have habitually proved illuminating and when it is in a position to know what it is talking about. The same is implied when we speak of the authority of the institutional church in matters of faith: the church, by God's grace, has been the effective medium of God's truth in the past and, as witness and keeper of holy writ, is in a position to be so still. But something else is implied in this case, too: that God, in his will to communicate the gospel to the ends of the earth, has *purposed* that the church should fulfil this task. The word of God has created around itself the structure of an attentive and communicative church. The gospel is not indifferent to its own communication; it has its dynamic of self-communication within itself, it is a wisdom that addresses and summons mankind (for in God the authority of command and the authority of truth are one), and so confers authority upon its witness not only *post factum*, by confirming the truth of its teaching, but *ante factum* by eliciting it.

Yet nothing in this affects the fact that when the church fails in its task, when it refuses to order its teaching in obedience to Scripture or wilfully imposes its own self-posited authority in defiance of Scripture, then it loses the authority which it was meant to possess. The example of a commentator who expounds a text is helpful because it is simple and paradigmatic; but it also fits well with what the Reformers thought that church teaching ought to be. In a loose sense all church teaching is expository — though there are movements of theological thought which are not themselves strictly expository, but which build upon the expository foundations (and to these we shall return shortly). Article 20 is content to put this in a negative form: theological reasoning which defies the force of exposition, or which exploits an irresponsible hermeneutic, cannot carry the authority which God wills that the teaching church should possess. Such was the case, the English Reformers judged, with the doctrines and practices listed in Article 22. The church's authority never floats free of Scripture, and can never be posited independently of Scripture, as though it could dispense with its text and establish its own commentary irrespective of what the text contained. At every point the church's authority conforms to the rule which we have spelled out for teaching authority in general: it consists in making the truth appear, in illuminating the reality which is the only judge of its effectiveness. It cannot be effective when the text contradicts it; it cannot be effective when it ceases to care whether the text contradicts it or not. The institutional church can forfeit its teaching authority (not for ever, to be sure, but in any given circumstance and at any given time), and by no other means can it forfeit it so thoroughly as by positing it on a false and absolutist basis.

Yet it is not unimportant that the Article expresses the church's obligation to Scripture negatively, and does not say that any teaching of the church must be positively authenticated by Scripture. This touches upon the freedom of Christian thought to 'develop' by theological reflection. The mediaeval church had achieved a rich expansion of the content of the Christian faith, going far beyond what had been taught in the patristic period, though already in the patristic period there were significant advances on the New Testament. In order to treat of this topic we ought to distinguish rather carefully two different kinds of development. There are developments that attempt to *elucidate* given understandings of the faith — for example, the Augustinian theory of original sin — and advances which *speculate* in the hope of drawing out the implications of Christian belief for other matters — for example, the doctrine of the immaculate conception of the Virgin Mary. Now, the Reformers do not rule out either of these kinds of thought as such. A biblical epistemology does not mean that thought must stand still. We have to grasp, appropriate, interpret and understand, and then we have to apply what we have learned to new problems.

What is, however, excluded in the last sentence of Article 20 is the confusion of Christian speculation with the fundamental message of the faith itself, in such a way that, in order to be accepted as a Christian in good standing, someone is required to assent to this or that result of Christian speculative thought. To take a modern example. It is legitimate for the church to apply the principles of biblical anthropology to the modern question about abortion, and to teach (in the light both of biblical anthropology and genetic science) that the foetus in the womb is an individual human being, deserving of protection. It may even be proper for the church, because of the grave social seriousness of the issue, to make it a matter of moral discipline that no member should have, encourage or perform an abortion. But it must not say to anyone: if you do not believe what we teach about the unborn child you are disobedient to the word of God. It cannot censure dissident *opinion* on the matter, because it is not a matter on which the text of Scripture teaches anything directly. It must always expose its reasoning to open discussion, so that the movement of thought, from exposition to speculation, can be tested for its adequacy.

Article 21, on the "general" or ecumenical councils, then tackles the question of the *elucidatory* advances in church doctrine, and here (despite the sceptical tone of the Article) the Reformers are in fact more permissive to the church. They themselves have commended the three creeds, the Nicene, Athanasian and Apostles', in Article 8 — and they will require as a condition for confirmation in the Church of England that the candidate knows the Lord's Prayer and the Decalogue (which are in the Scriptures) and the Apostles' Creed and the Catechism (which are not). There is a place, in other words, for the church's use of the "power of the keys" — the admission or exclusion of individuals from the fellowship of believers — in respct to some other formulations than those of the actual text of Scripture. But these things must be shown to be "taken out of" Scripture, i.e. they must express doctrines which are so clearly present (though perhaps in other words) that it would be impossible to dissent from them without dissenting from Scripture itself. There is a need, therefore, for the church's "definition" of its doctrine, so that it can clarify for itself and those to whom it ministers what is, and what it not, Christian faith. But no definition is so hallowed by age, universal acceptance, or by the formal ecumenicity of the Council which promulgated it, that it is in principle no longer dependent upon Scripture for its validity. Not the Apostles' Creed, not the Thirty Nine Articles, not the *homoousion* itself. The question, "Is it true to Scripture?" is never impertinent or irrelevant, and the church, for its own integrity's sake, must constantly satisfy itself of the adequacy of its norms of belief by the biblical measure.

Let us pause here for a moment and consider the picture that has been set before us. The church stands under the apostolic testimony and is obligated by the apostolic testimony. Why? Because the church is created by the apostolic testimony. To be the church is to be moulded by that testimony, to live within it and by it. The testimony does not simply represent a series of dogmatic limitations beyond which thought is forbidden to stray: it is the very lifeblood of Christian thought — it evokes it and demands it. Christian speculation is not *tolerated* by the testimony — it is *required* if that testimony is to fashion every part of the church's life and attitude. Therefore we must speak of the church's complete freedom of thought. It may think about anything, and with any intellectual aids. It does not have to be fearful of philosophical terminology, of speculative questions, of scientific discovery, just so long as this freedom is the gospel freedom created by the propulsive power of the apostolic testimony working within the church's mind at the instigation of the Spirit. We say that the church stands "under" Scripture — but that preposition is not to suggest a crushing weight, as when a rider lies under his horse after a fall. It is under Scripture as the earth is under the sky, the sun and the rain. It is fructified by it; its life and its produce are given in response to it; its health and strength depend upon it.

All this we have been able to say without reference to church order. It is not from its organization that the church derives its authority, but from its adherence to the apostolic word. Yet this does not make the organization unnecessary. We recall what we said in Chapter 7 about the relation of institutional churches to the catholic church. The church is not the institutions, but the institutions are the structural expressions of the church, and indicate its determination to continue being the church and to perform the task it has been given. Christians are Christians, and so members of the catholic church, before they organize themselves as institutional churches; but it is precisely because they take being Christians seriously that they do organize themselves as institutional churches.

We say "organize themselves", which, of course, is what they do. But the phrase might suggest that the impulse towards order came entirely from man's side, or at least that the decisions about what form the order should take were entirely human decisions. It might seem that it hardly mattered how Christians organized themselves, provided that they organized themselves somehow. This doctrine, which is Erastian in inspiration, has commended itself to some Protestant churches, especially congregationalist ones. But it is mistaken. It is not the doctrine of Article 34, which says, not that all aspects of church order "may be changed according to the diversities of countries, times and men's manners" but that "traditions and ceremonies" may, "so that nothing be ordained against God's Word" — a position that may be described, not inaccurately but perhaps misleadingly, as "semi-Erastian". It is clear from the content of

Articles 22-24 that there are some points of practice and order which are not negotiable in a church where the role of church order is rightly understood in relation to the church's authority and responsibility to teach the word of God.

This is to say that the authoritative proclamation of God's word, though distinct from the governing authority of any given church structure, nevertheless demands that there shall be certain elements of church structure which will appear in any obedient church. It is not that the church is given the gospel and then has untrammelled freedom to find means to fulfil its task of communicating and cherishing it. Rather, some means are implied in the truth of the gospel itself, which demands to be communicated and cherished in a certain way. The structures of governing authority within the church, therefore, are still beholden to the authority of the gospel which the church teaches — just as structures of government in society are beholden to the moral authority of justice. Yet the authority of social institutions is not the *same* as the moral authority of justice, and neither is the authority of church institutions the same as the authority of the truth. The word of God shapes the order of the church. The phrase "organize themselves" must be complemented by another: Christian believers *find themselves ordered* in a certain form of society precisely by the message which they believe and are charged to proclaim. And the decisive character of their order, as the Reformers understand it, is that it maintains the teaching of the truth of the gospel. The truth of the gospel is a self-communicating truth, which reaches out into the world; the church which it fashions is a church of authoritative communication, which maintains, by its structures, the central position of the New Testament gospel as the norm of faith.

It is in this context that the Articles approach the question of ordained ministry within the church (Article 23).

The context is striking, in the first place, for what it tells us about their view of the ministry. Ordained ministry was a ministry of the word of God, an exercise of the teaching authority which is indispensible to the church's being. The most significant modification which Cranmer made to the service for the ordination of priests was to replace the pious custom by which the ordinand was handed eucharistic vessels with the solemn presentation of a Bible, accompanied by the words "Take thou authority to preach the word of God, and to minister the holy sacraments in this congregation, where thou shalt be so appointed." The priesthood, as Anglicans first conceived it, was to be a preaching ministry as well as a sacramental ministry. It was not primarily an administrative role. It should not even be described as "leadership" unless we remember that leadership in the church is exercised only in obedience and service to the life-giving gospel. That is why only those should be admitted to it who have shown themselves to be people whom the gospel has grasped and transformed, and why serious theological study is a prerequisite for ministry in all churches descended from the Reformation.

But if the context says something important about the nature of the ministry, it also says something important about the structures of the church. Once again, the order in which things occur is illuminating. Why do we treat of the ministry in this context, but defer discussion of the consecration of bishops until Article 36? Because the question of the episcopacy is a matter of discretionary order and the question of consecration a matter of rites and ceremonies. But ordained ministry as such stands on a very different footing. The two marks of the church which were stipulated in Article 19 are made the basis of a single form of required order: ministry of word and sacrament. The formulation of Article 23 carefully avoids construing this ordained ministry specifically in terms of the threefold order of bishops, priests and deacons; neither does it allude to the succession of orders which maintains continuity with the earliest church. To neither of these things were Elizabethan churchmen, at least, indifferent; yet in stating what they thought essential to the order of any church, they were content to stipulate nothing more than an ordained ministry of word and sacrament.

How are we to assess their conception of the matter? We can admire the way in which the distinction between the essential and the inessential is made, and we can admire the determination to confine that which is essential in church order to the demands of word and sacrament, thus subordinating order to the life-centre of the church and forbidding it to take on an autonomous life of its own. Yet there are questions which ought to be put to the Reformers about the schema which results. First, the identification of essential church order with the existence of an ordained ministry: is there not something which should be said prior to this — and said quite distinctly within the context of church order — namely, that *every* member of the church participates in the authority given to the church to proclaim and witness to the death and resurrection of Christ? That ·the Holy Spirit's distribution of gifts of service upon all believers is a factor of church order which comes before the differentiation of the "pastoral" ministries of episcopal discipline and diaconal service? And that this total mutual ministry is nothing other than a ministry of the *word*, all of it, though not all of it is properly carried out by preaching? Can we speak of church *order*, in other words, without first speaking of the way in which every member of the church is ordained to minister the word of God to others, before we go on to speak of a differentiated and chosen ministry, set apart from this universal ministry, for the defence of the truth and the strengthening of witness? To talk of church order ought, from the beginning, to be to talk of the unity and mutuality of the church's members in Christ, and of how they order themselves together.

We cannot accuse the Reformers, certainly, of being indifferent to the dynamic relation between priest and people, of favouring the creation of a church within a church. They remind us in Article 24 that the ordained ministry is for the benefit of the whole people of God and is not self-justifying in isolation from them. The ordained minister must be a communicator as well as a learned man — that is implied in his being a teacher. He is the vehicle of a message which he must, of course, have understood and been gripped intellectually by, but he must be able to "teach others also" (2 Tim. 2:2). And this means that all ministry must be, in principle, comprehensible. The clergy of today should not take this as an invitation to speak in baby-talk, or to offer little children's addresses to adult congregations. They must pass on God's word to others, as they themselves received it, as something to evoke the most sustained intellectual worship. Nevertheless, meaningless obstacles to communication must be removed — and the most important of these, to the English Reformers, was the sentimental attachment that many English Christians of their time had to the Latin tongue — including many Christians who could not understand it. All this the English Reformers grasped with a clarity for which we have continued cause to be grateful. Yet they did not, we must confess, reformulate their conception of church order radically enough around the fundamental mutuality of service, a mutuality which in no way detracts from what needs also to be said about the ordained ministry.

In the second place, we must ask whether they have adequately conceived the ministry as a *responsive* movement to the dynamic force of the word of God. Is it not a very passive treasure, this treasure of word and sacrament, waiting, as it were, to be protected, maintained, distributed by a ministry which serves it, but which is not, nevertheless, really conceived as shaped and held in being by it? And does this weakness not reflect that earlier failure of the Articles to say anything about the catholic church? Have they not failed already to tell us that the church is present wherever the word of God is heard and Christ confessed, that the word is not protected in the church like a jewel in a box, but rather creates the church around it as it strikes out on its own adventures? And does this not mean that their conception of church order is too arbitrary? If they had wrestled further with this question which they broached, the question of overcoming the positivism of church order, might we not have had from them a subtly different treatment of the relationship of word and sacrament? For in the celebration of the sacraments we see the church already ordered — not diffused and "invisible", but formed and shaped into a worshipping community. And in the celebration of the sacraments we see (as patristic tradition knew) a word spoken in action, not something *other* than the reading and the preaching of the gospel, but an acted accompaniment to it which belongs to the ministry of the word inseparably. Ought we not to see in the sacraments a middle-term between faith and order, which marks the church's first and foundational concretion into a historical body living in faith? But already we have found the path which leads our thoughts from teaching to the sacraments, and we must not hurry precipitately along it, but follow it in good time in the company of the guides whom we have chosen to lead us.

10

THE SACRAMENTS
(Articles 25-31)

When the English Reformers write about the sacraments, they are on their home ground. Much of their intellectual energy — of Cranmer in particular this is true — was poured into controversy about the eucharist. We may be disappointed that it was so. Why was there no English equivalent to the great Bible commentaries of Luther and Calvin? Why no leading soteriological theme, to play the role that justification played among the Lutherans? Why no synoptic view of Christian doctrine, reviving the tradition of the mediaeval *summa*, such as the Reformed churches attempted? But there it is — the peculiar minor genius of the English Reformation. It left a Prayer Book and a church constitution, with literature to provide a theological rationale for the one, and to justify the other against its detractors. It was limited work, but solid; and we are still dependent upon it. It did not free subsequent generations, of course, from controversy about the eucharist. Yet it determined, within fairly narrow limits, the ground on which that controversy would be pursued. Contrast Cranmer's Article 'Of the Lord's Supper', which denies 'the real and bodily presence (as they term it) of Christ's flesh and blood in the sacrament of the Lord's Supper', with the Elizabethan Article 28, which says instead that the body of Christ is eaten "after an heavenly and spiritual manner", and there you have the principle alternative paths open to Anglican eucharistic thought for three centuries or more.

For this reason I propose, in this "conversation" with Tudor Christianity, to keep a distance on the details of its sacramental theology, and to ask, more generally, what was implied in its approach to the subject. For we should not take it for granted that any systematic Christian theology will include a section on the sacraments. The word itself, after all, has undergone two radical shifts of meaning within the history of Christian thought: from its use in the New Testament (where *musterion* means a "secret", especially the secret purposes of God revealed in Jesus) to its incorporation by the patristic age into a general theory of *signs*; and from that again to the mediaeval conception of a stated number of Christian *rituals* with a common structure, which mediate divine grace. Leaving aside the extreme possibility — realized in some Protestant groups — that the eucharist and baptism might cease to be practised altogether, there is still more than one way of organizing theological reflection upon them. One might try to do without a unifying concept, and treat baptism and the eucharist separately. Or one might revive the patristic thought that they were two among a much larger number of diverse signs of the operation of the divine within the material world — a train of thought which has had some popularity in our own century. Or one might accept the mediaeval project of identifying a stated number of authoritative rituals in principle, but try to implement it differently. This third way, in my own view, is what was, and still is required. The way the Reformers took was none of these. They defended as much of the developed scholastic doctrine of the sacraments as they could, and altered it only when they felt they had to. The difficulties and incoherencies which their sacramentology so often raises are usually attributable to their tenderness in guarding the shape of scholastic doctrine, while introducing what were, in effect, wrecking amendments. The sacraments, then, are one of the three great pillars of the mediaeval doctrine of grace (the others being justification and predestination) which the Reformers inherited and attempted to pass on in revised form. The passing-on was more successful in this case than in the other two, the revision more hesitant.

Let us go back to their central theme, which inspires every revision which they wished to make: "The offering of Christ once made, is the perfect redemption, propitiation, and satisfaction for all the sins of the whole world, both original and actual, and there is none other satisfaction for sin, but that alone" (Art. 31). They would not have known what it meant to say that their concern was "eschatological", but that in truth is what it was. The "once for all" of the Epistle to the Hebrews determines the shape of history: it declares that Christ is its climax and completion, in which redemption is totally present and to which nothing remains to be added — save for the final "appearing". What was alarming about the mediaeval doctrine of grace was its tendency to suggest some kind of advance upon the achievement of Christ's passion. Christ could all too easily cease to be regarded as the completion of things, and become an intermediate step to something else, whether something apart from the realm of the historical or something superseding within history itself.

We recall that Cranmer concluded his forty two Articles with four

on the Last Things, which brought the eschatological motif to explicit
statement. The first of these denied that "the Resurrection of the dead
is . . . yet brought to pass" — which would imply (in Cranmer's view)
that it "only belonged to the soul". We would then be talking of a gnostic
redemption *out* of history, not a redemption *of* history. Yet if we swing
to the opposite pole of materialism, his second Article warned us, and
affirm that souls "die with the bodies", we are denying that the
resurrection *of Christ* has brought life from the dead to pass, and we
make of eternal life a mere unrealized hope, still concealed within the
womb of the future. We must say that life from the dead is *present*
in the risen Christ, and that the resurrection of all the dead must *follow*
— and yet not follow as a necessity immanent within history itself,
but simply as the implication of his accomplishment. Unless the dialectic
between the accomplished end of history and the immanent shapeless-
ness of historical events is sustained, then Christ becomes, as it were,
swallowed up into history, reduced to the status of a merely formative
figure, "noteworthy", as Kierkegaard complained about the Hegelian
view, "because of his consequences". And this was the ground for
Cranmer's third eschatological Article, attacking the doctrine of world-
perfecting historical "stages" which was the legacy of Joachim of Fiore,
the "heretics called Millenarii" who "cast themselves headlong into a
Jewish dotage".

    The fourth and last Article was the most important. It denied "the
dangerous opinion that all men, be they never so ungodly, shall at length
be saved, when they have suffered pains for their sins a certain time".
Why was this denial necessary? Why should it be "dangerous" to
assert the salvation of all, which is (as some would argue) no more
than to attribute universality to the effects of Christ's atonement? We
may note in passing that Cranmer (quite properly) advanced no
opinion on whether any member of mankind would in fact be utterly
condemned — a matter which must, in every case, rest with God. But
he reacted sharply to the pretension to know that none would be. For
such an opinion has hedged its bets about Christ. It has claimed
universal *effects* for the atonement, right enough, but only out of a
certain nervousness that the atonement *itself* has not achieved true
universality. What is God's love to do, it has asked itself, if Christ has
failed to incorporate the whole of mankind in his representative
triumph? Why, then, those who have slipped through this net must be
caught in another one! But it is not in that spirit that God has offered
us his Son to represent us — not so as to leave it to *us* to decide
whether Christ shall in fact be the last Adam or not. There before
Pontius Pilate was that new mankind, there and nowhere else. No
choice of ours can enhance or detract from the universality of that
figure; no subsequent refusal can turn the future of redemption into

another course. The question that is asked of us in our time is not: shall all mankind, then, be saved in Christ? — for that question has been answered by him in his time, and does not need the living of our lives to answer it further. The question is this: shall we ourselves be saved with all mankind in Christ? For if we refuse and are lost, we have carried away no part of mankind with us to perdition, we have recorded no dissenting votes. Our time is of itself nothing, and represents nothing; but between the living of our lives and that eclipse of our time into nothingness, God has set his time, the day of Jesus's resurrection.

To return, then, to the cardinal assertion of Article 31: there is no *other* grace available to mankind than that offering once made. History cannot generate any other, not by building upon it, not by improving it, not by imitating it. And not, the Reformers wish to tell us, by *repeating* it, thereby denying it its sovereignty over history and absorbing it into the cyclical patterns out of which our time is spun. It is not easy for us to sympathize with the intensity of their reaction to this thought — but that is because in the modern West we do not first of all think of time as cyclical, as our ancestors did. For us the more immediate thought is that of progress, and the more pressing danger is of viewing Christ's death nostalgically, as something we have gone beyond. Yet, as the example of Nietzsche warns us, historicism reverts easily enough to cyclical conceptions when it becomes self-critical. We need not ask now whether the idea of repeated sacrifice in the Eucharist can be successfully qualified, so as to safeguard it against the loss of the "once for all" — though such a question is important to ecumenical discussion. To understand the Reformers it is enough that we hear their warning and sense with them the danger. Our salvation is wrought for us in the death and resurrection of a first-century man — not strung out week by week in ritual representation through history, which is to make God the prisoner of time rather than its master. When Cranmer insisted (in his Article on the Lord's Supper) that "because Christ was taken up into heaven, and there shall continue unto the end of the world, a faithful man ought not, either to believe, or openly to confess the real, and bodily presence . . . of Christ's flesh and blood" his interest in invoking the ascension was just this: to protect the triumph of God's Messiah against the constant undoing and doing again which is implicit in ritual repetition. And the Elizabethan Bishop Guest, when he wrote (in terms congenial to Calvin's disciples as well as to Catholic Anglicans) of the body "given, taken, and eaten . . . after an heavenly and spiritual manner" (Article 28) had intended that these words should be set beside a similar proclamation of Christ's ascension into heaven, stronger, if anything, than Cranmer's: "from there *and nowhere else* (as Augustine says) to come to judge the quick and the dead."

The sacraments, then, mediate to us, in our time, the decisive redemption of mankind by Christ in his. He is *present* to us — of course! for how else could we be part of his representative humanity? But this does not come about by his being imprisoned in the necessities — cyclical or progressive — of our time, but rather by our liberation to be united with him in his. The sacrament represents that first-century event to us, and binds us into the reality of that first-century event. "I am crucified with Christ" (Gal. 2:20). This is, needless to say, not a Zwinglian doctrine of the sacraments. The Zwinglian theory marks a half-way point in the reformation of sacramental theology, at which it had become clear what the Reformers would have to *deny* about the sacraments, but not what they would have to *affirm*; so that it seemed possible that everything necessary could be said about the sacramental presence of Christ in terms of mental recollection and memory. But such a formulation entirely failed to get to the root of the issue, which is Christ's eschatological presence to us. It is subject to exactly the same criticism as the mediaeval doctrine — namely that it absolutizes the gulf between our time and Christ's, and so denies to his time that immediate authority over our time which belongs to it as the Last Time and to him as the Last Adam. Not even of Article 29 (refused a place in the Articles of 1563 out of nervousness for Catholic-leaning sensibilities) can it correctly be said that it is at all Zwinglian in inspiration. For the point made in that Article is simply that the reality of the sacrament is nothing other than the redemptive presence of Christ. The unreality of the wicked communicant's participation is not a matter of *his* failure to conjure up the memories and moral dispositions which the believer has successfully conjured up; rather, it is the refusal of Christ to give himself to unbelief. For the very nature of the sacrament is that in it Christ gives himself, really, to faith.

This brings us to the greatest formal revision which the Reformers introduced into the mediaeval sacramentology: the reduction in the number of sacraments which they acknowledge, from seven to two. This may, on the face of it, seem to be merely a formal point, to be considered only after the general conception of the sacraments has been established; but in fact it is of central importance for their understanding of what a sacrament is. For the figure seven was reached under a number of converging constraints, many of them arbitrary, of which one was a desire to interpret the sacraments biographically, in terms of the life-career of the Christian pilgrim. From birth (baptism) through growth to maturity (confirmation), by nourishment (eucharist) and healing from disorder (penance), in the service of the community by leadership (ordination) and by propagation (marriage), to final cleansing and preparation for glory (extreme unction), the sacraments were to accompany the believer at every stage along his way[1].

Nothing could more strikingly illustrate the orientation of the mediaeval concept of grace than this conformity of the doctrine of the sacraments to a doctrine of the seven ages of man. It was, of course, also said (and proved with some deviousness of exegesis) that the seven sacraments were each instituted by Christ; but this criterion carried little weight in effect. The Reformers elevated the principle of dominical institution to the status of a critical canon, and on the strength of it rejected (after some hesitations about penance) all but two — a decision that is made more clearly in the Elizabethan Article 25 than in the corresponding Edwardian Article. In so doing they wished to assert that the grace of God (in the sacraments, as in any other form) was nothing other than union with Jesus Christ.

But did they assert it effectively? It is easy to see the direction in which they intended to move; yet the simple claim that "there are two sacraments ordained of Christ our Lord in the gospel" hardly takes them far enough. Why should the Lord's command be more weighty than his practice and the practice of the apostles? If the laying-on of hands is viewed as *one* ritual rather than the three which it had become by the late middle ages, can we plausibly deny it dominical authorization? And should they not have gone further than counting dominical practices and commands, to ask whether some rituals stood in a specially significant relation to the saving events themselves, as they well understood the eucharist to stand to the crucifixion? "The Supper of the Lord", we read (Art. 28), "is not only a sign of the love that Christians ought to have among themselves one to another: but rather it is a sacrament of our redemption by Christ's death." But when we turn back to the comparable assertion about baptism, deliberately conceived as a complement to it (Art. 27), we read no more than this: "Baptism is not only a sign of profession, and mark of difference, whereby Christian men are discerned from other that be not christened, but is also a sign of regeneration or new birth." What is needed is some comparable assertion about the relationship of baptism to *Christ*: it is a sacrament of our redemption by his advent, since it was in the waters of baptism that he was revealed to us as the anointed Son of God. And may we not say something similar about the laying-on of hands and the ascension? And even about the keeping of the Lord's Day and the resurrection? These questions, which cannot be developed in this context but must wait for another occasion, are

---

[1]. Cf. St. Thomas, *Summa Theologiae* III q.65 a.7.

raised merely in order to show what a thoroughly Christocentric account of sacramental grace would demand: not simply that it is Christ who is present to us in the sacraments, not simply that it is Christ's command that authorizes them, but that the formal differentiation of sacramental grace into seven, two, or (shall we even dare to say?) four sacraments must be authorized by the formal articulation of the Christ-event itself. We cannot establish the figure two by a simple process of fault-finding which disqualifies, one after the other, five out of Peter Lombard's arbitrarily selected seven.

But this leads us to a further point which Cranmer, with his characteristic flash of intuition, had understood but which the Elizabethans missed; and that is the relationship of sacramental grace, both in its undifferentiated and in its differentiated aspect, to the church. The Elizabethan Article 25 begins with words which, borrowed from the Augsburg Confession, had formed the conclusion of the Edwardian Article: "Sacraments ordained of Christ, be not only badges or tokens of Christian men's profession, but rather they be certain sure witnesses, and effectual signs of grace, and God's good will towards us . . ." Since these words formed the model for the opening sentences of the Articles on baptism and the eucharist, there was a certain neatness in transferring them to the head of the Article. But Cranmer had begun differently: "Our Lord Jesus Christ hath knit together a company of new people with sacraments . . .", and with that reference to the company of new people had supplied something that was lacking both in the mediaeval tradition of thought about the sacraments and in most of what the Reformation had made of it. Why *sacramental* grace? Why should the blessings of the gospel be made present to us in *this* form too, since they are so strongly present in the reading and preaching of the apostolic word? Because the effect of the gospel is to knit together a company of new people. With this answer, had it been given the attention it deserved, the Reformation might have broken free of the shackles of individualism which had bound the mediaeval doctrine of grace.

But what it needed was a doctrine of the church; and that, as we have seen, neither Cranmer nor the Elizabethans were ready to supply. Had Cranmer's seed-thought been allowed to develop, there could have emerged an exciting doctrine of the church, and a doctrine of the sacraments which fully belonged to it. The sacraments would have been understood as the communal dimension of the gospel word, giving the church a twofold, sevenfold or (shall we say?) fourfold mark of identity — baptism, eucharist, the Lord's Day and the laying-on of hands — which was formed by the apostolic proclamation of Jesus: made known as the Christ, he suffered, rose and ascended to the right hand of power on high. And they would have been understood, too, as the foundations of church order, knitting together the company of new people and setting before it its fourfold task of witness, suffering, cherishing of ordered life and prayer for the Kingdom of God. But, again, this sketch must wait for another opportunity. It is not our privilege, in conversation with Tudor Christianity, to force upon it the answers that we would give ourselves, but merely to show the gap that is left, leaving the doctrine of the sacraments without a proper home within the scheme of things, tacked uneasily onto the section on the authority of the divine word in church-order, and lacking an account of the catholic church in which to find its proper situation.

But we can go further, and say that Cranmer's momentary glimpse of the relation between sacraments and the catholic church could have supplied not only what is needed in *any* understanding of the sacraments, but what was needed quite specifically in the *Reformers'* understanding.

Constantly we find them situated in apparent discomfort between objectivity and subjectivity: the objectivity which must be ascribed to sacramental grace, and the subjectivity implied in the role of faith in appropriating it. The sacraments "be not only badges or tokens of Christian men's profession, but rather they be certain sure witnesses and effectual signs of grace and God's good will towards us, by the which he doth work invisibly in us". The whole tone of the treatment is set by that strong statement; the addition of the epithets *certa* to the Augsburg Confessions's *testimonia*, and *efficacia* to its *signa*, show the way in which the English Reformers intended to be understood, deliberately echoing the scholastic *efficiunt quod figurant*. Yet this strong assertion of objective effect is qualified in Article 28, when we read that "to such as rightly, worthily, and with faith receive the same" the bread is a sharing of Christ's body and the wine of his blood. The implications of this phrase were spelled out in the Elizabethan Article 29, "Of the Wicked which do not eat the Body of Christ in the use of the Lord's Supper". Unbelieving communicants do not partake of Christ, but "rather to their condemnation do eat and drink the sign or sacrament of so great a thing", a conclusion which certainly assumes *objectivity* of a kind, but not exactly objective *grace.*.

The difficulty which the Reformers faced lay, of course, in the mediaeval doctrine of the sacraments itself, which, while never, actually or in intent, denying the indispensability of faith to salvation, so conceived the objective operation of sacramental grace as to make faith appear as a necessary result of it. Now, there is nothing wrong with speaking of faith as the "necessary result" of grace (though such a phrase has, of course, to be understood in a non-mechanistic sense). The very concept of the prevenience of grace might even be thought to demand it. The Zwinglian alternative was to make faith autonomous, and so return to the objectionable Pelagianizing concepts of grace as congruent or condign which the Reformers repudiated. What the conservative Reformers found unsatisfactory was the attribution of faith to *sacramental* grace as such rather than to the proclamation of the gospel. "Faith comes by hearing, and hearing by the word of Christ" (Rom. 10:17). Although the scholastic doctrine had attempted to retain the association of word and action in the sacrament, the way in which it did so was too weak: the word (e.g. the baptismal formula, or the words of institution) served only to *define* the sacramental action and not to provide a spearhead of proclamation to which faith could attach itself. At the heart, then, of the Reformers' concern with the subjectivity of belief is a concern not for individual autonomy but for the primacy of the word. To allow sacramental grace *ex opere operato* (as they understood that phrase) was to allow ritual performance to supplant the gospel word from its commanding position as the determining factor in the church's existence. What they needed was a conception of the objective power of the ritual which would not threaten, implicitly or explicitly, the primacy of the hearing of the word of Christ.

Once we grasp the problem in this light, we can appreciate that the simultaneous attribution of objectivity and subjectivity to the effects of the sacrament is not necessarily self-contradictory or vacillating. Everything depends on what effects we are talking about. The Reformers wished to say that the sacraments could not substitute for the gospel in providing a primary ground for faith. If someone believed, it was because the gospel had aroused faith within his heart; if someone disbelieved the gospel, no pious attention to the sacramental act could compensate. That having been understood, we can also say that performance of the sacraments gives a *concrete public form* in which the gospel is made known and does its work, not only quickening faith but strengthening and confirming it. Though attendance at the sacraments is, alas, compatible with unbelief, the normal and normative function of the sacrament is as a proclamation of the gospel, and it is as such that the effects of proclamation can be confidently ascribed to it.

In such an account we lack only the rationale for the distinctive sacramental form of proclamation; and the answer must be that in the sacrament the word first displays its power to gather the believing community in common confession of faith. It is by *defining the community* that the sacrament carries the preaching of the word forward, and divides objectively between belief and unbelief. Are we to say, then, that the sacramental community is without its ambiguities, that it perfectly represents the eschatological company of the redeemed? Certainly not — and, of course, no orthodox Catholic could have claimed this. Yet the sacramental community *does* represent the eschatological company, even if not perfectly. It does present us with the challenge of the gospel in a social form, through which we can see the city of God. It does, therefore, excite our faith and condemn our faithlessness. The grace of the sacrament is objective in the sense that the eschatological community is present there, though veiled and ambiguous. Whether the sacrament means salvation to *us* will depend on how we receive it, and cannot be concluded automatically either from our formal participation or from our formal absence. But it is nevertheless mankind's *salvation* that is made present there, and that objectively.

The end has broken into history, and is proclaimed to us in the word of Christ. And the firstfruits of that proclamation are the fragmentary signs of the new humanity, met in Christ's name to live in the power of his coming, his death, his resurrection and his triumph. There we see the approaching city of God. We can no more wish it into neutrality by our unbelief than we can, by closing our eyes, avert the end of all things.

Appendix 1

The Forty Two Articles (1553)
The Thirty Nine Articles (1571)

SOURCES OF TEXTS

The text of the Forty Two Articles and of the Thirty Nine Articles is reproduced from Charles Hardwick, *A History of the Articles of Religion* (Cambridge: John Deighton, 1851). The text of two chapters from the Westminster Confession is from *The Confession of Faith and Catechisms agreed upon by the Assembly of Divines at Westminster* (London: Robert Bostock, 1650). Quotations from the Edwardian Book of Common Prayer are taken from *The First and Second Prayer Books of King Edward VI* (London: Dent, Everyman's Library, 1910). Documents of the continental Reformation and of the Council of Trent are quoted from Philip Schaff, *Creeds of Christendom* (New York: Harper, 1877. Repr. Grand Rapids: Baker, 1977). The orthography of all quotations used in the book has been modernised, but the Appendices reproduce the original forms.

THE FORTY-TWO ARTICLES (1553)

I
Of faith in the holie Trinitie.

There is but one liuing, and true God, and he is euerlasting, with out bodie, partes, or passions, of infinite power, wisedome, and goodnesse, the maker, and preseruer of all thinges bothe visible, and inuisible, and in vnitie of this Godhead there bee three persones of one substaunce, power, and eternitie, the Father, the Soonne, and the holie Ghoste,

II
That the worde, or Sonne of God, was made a very man.

The sonne whiche is the woorde of the father, tooke mannes nature in the wombe of the blessed virgine Marie of her Substaunce, so that two hole, and perfeicte natures, that is to saie, the Godhead, and manhode were ioigned together into one persone, neuer to be diuided, wherof is one Christe very God, and very manne, who truely suffred, was crucified, dead, and buried, to reconcile his father to vs, and to be a Sacrifice for all sinne of manne, bothe originall, and actuall.

III
Of the goyng doune of Christe into Helle.

As Christ died, and was buried for vs: so also it is to be beleued, that he went downe in to hell. For the bodie laie in the Sepulchre, untill the resurrection: but his Ghoste departing from him, was with the Ghostes

THE THIRTY-NINE ARTICLES (1571)

I
Of fayth in the holy Trinitie

There is but one lyuyng and true God, euerlastyng, without body, partes, or passions, of infinite power, wysdome, and goodnesse, the maker and preseruer of al things both visible and inuisible. And in vnitie of this Godhead there be three persons, of one substaunce, power, and eternitie, the father, the sonne, and the holy ghost.

II
Of the worde or sonne of God which was made very man.

The Sonne, which is the worde of the Father, begotten from euerlastyng of the Father, the very and eternall GOD, of one substaunce with the father, toke mans nature in the wombe of the blessed Virgin, of her substaunce: so that two whole and perfect natures, that is to say the Godhead and manhood, were ioyned together in one person, neuer to be diuided, whereof is one Christe, very GOD and very man, who truely suffered, was crucified, dead, and buried, to reconcile his father to vs, and to be a sacrifice, not only for originall gylt, but also for all actuall sinnes of men.

III
Of the goyng downe of Christe into hell.

As Christe dyed for vs, and was buryed: so also it is to be beleued that he went downe into hell.

that were in prison, or in Helle, and didde preache to the same, as the place of S. Peter dooeth testifie.

IV
The Resurrection of Christe.
Christe didde truelie rise againe from deathe, and tooke again his bodie with flesh, bones, and all thinges apperteining to the perfection of mannes nature, wherewith he ascended into Heauen, and there sitteth, untill he retourne to iudge men at the last daie.

IV
Of the Resurrection of Christe.
Christe dyd truely aryse agayne from death, and toke agayne his body, with flesh, bones, and all thinges apparteyning to the perfection of mans nature, wherewith he ascended into heauen, and there sitteth, vntyll he returne to iudge all men at the last day.

V
Of the holy ghost.
The holy ghost, proceedyng from the father and the sonne, is of one substaunce, maiestie, and glorie, with the father and the sonne, very and eternall God.

V
The doctrine of holie Scripture is sufficient to Saluation
Holie Scripture conteineth all thinges necessarie to Saluation: So that whatsoeuer is neither read therein, nor maie be proued therby, although it be somtime receiued of the faithful, as Godlie, and profitable for an ordre, and comelinesse: Yeat no manne ought to bee constreigned to beleue it, as an article of faith, or repute it requisite to the necessitie of Saluation.

VI
Of the sufficiencie of the holy Scriptures for saluation.
Holye Scripture conteyneth all thinges necessarie to saluation: so that whatsoeuer is not read therein, nor may be proued therby, is not to be required of anye man, that it shoulde be beleued as an article of the fayth, or be thought requisite as necessarie to saluation.

In the name of holy Scripture, we do vnderstande those Canonicall bookes of the olde and newe Testament, of whose aucthoritie was neuer any doubt in the Churche.
Of the names and number of the Canonicall Bookes.

Genesis.
Exodus.
Leuiticus.
Numerie.
Deuteronomium.
Iosue.
Iudges.

Ruth.
The .1. booke of Samuel.
The .2. booke of Samuel.
The .1. booke of Kinges.
The .2. booke of Kinges.
The .1. booke of Chroni.
The .2. booke of Chroni.
The .1. booke of Esdras.
The .2. booke of Esdras.
The booke of Hester.
The booke of Iob.
The Psalmes.
The Prouerbes.
Ecclesia. or preacher.
Cantica, or songes of Sa.
4. Prophetes the greater.
12. Prophetes the lesse.

And the other bookes, (as Hierome sayth) the Churche doth reade for example of lyfe and instruction of maners: but yet doth it not applie them to establishe any doctrine. Such are these followyng.
The third booke of Esdras.
The fourth booke of Esdras.
The booke of Tobias.
The booke of Iudith.
The rest of the booke of Hester.
The booke of Wisdome.
Iesus the sonne of Sirach.
Baruch, the prophet.
Song of the .3. Children.
The storie of Susanna.
Of Bel and the Dragon.
The prayer of Manasses.
The .1. booke of Machab.
The .2. booke of Macha.

All the bookes of the newe Testament, as they are commonly receaued, we do receaue and accompt them for Canonicall.

VI
The olde Testamente is not to be refused

The olde Testament is not to bee put awaie as though it were contrarie to the newe, but to be kept still: for bothe

VII
Of the Olde Testament.

The olde Testament is not contrary to the newe, for both in the olde and newe Testament euerlastyng lyfe is offered to mankynde by Christe, in the olde, and newe Testamentes, euerlasting life is offred to mankinde by Christ, who is the onelie mediatour betwene Godde and manne, being bothe Godde, and manne. Wherefore thei are not to be hearde, whiche feigne that the olde Fathers didde looke onely for transitorie promises.

who is the onlye mediatour betweene God and man, being both God and man. Wherefore they are not to be hearde whiche faigne that the olde fathers dyd looke onlye for transitorie promises. Although the lawe geuen from God by Moyses, as touchyng ceremonies and rites, do not bynde Christian men, nor the ciuile preceptes therof, ought of necessitie to be receaued in any common wealth: yet notwith-standyng, no Christian man whatsoeuer, is free from the obedience of the commaundementes, whiche are called morall.

VII
The three Credes
The three Credes, Nicene Crede, Athanasius Crede, and that whiche is commonlie called the Apostles Crede, ought throughly to be received : for thei maie be proued by most certeine warrauntes of holie Scripture.

VIII
Of originall or birthe sinne
Originall sinne standeth not in the folowing of Adam, as the Pellagianes doe vainelie talke, whiche also the Anabaptistes doe now a daies renue, but it is the fault, and corruption of the nature of euery manne, that naturallie is engendred of the ofspring of Adam, whereby manne is very farre gone from his former righteousnesse, whiche he had at his creation and is of his owne nature geuen to euill, so that the fleshe desireth alwaies contrarie to the spirit, and therefore in euery persone borne into this worlde, it deserueth Goddes wrath and damnation : And this infection of nature doeth remaine, yea in theim that are baptized, wherby the lust of the

VIII
Of the three Credes.
The three Credes, Nicene Crede, Athanasius Crede, and that whiche is commonlye called the Apostles' Crede, ought throughlye to be receaued and beleued: for they may be proued by moste certayne warrauntes of holye scripture.

IX
Of originall or birth sinne.
Originall sinne standeth not in the folowing of Adam (as the Pelagians do vaynely talke) but it is the fault and corruption of the nature of euery man, that naturally is engendred of the ofspring of Adam, whereby man is very farre gone from originall ryghteousnes, and is of his owne nature enclined to euyll, so that the fleshe lusteth alwayes contrary to the spirite, and therefore in euery person borne into this worlde, it deserueth Gods wrath and damnation. And this infection of nature doth remayne, yea in them that are re-generated, whereby the luste of the fleshe called in Greke φρόνημα σαρκὸς, (whiche some do expoune, the wisedome, some sensualitie, some

fleshe called in Greke φρόνημα σαρκὸς, (whiche some do expoune, the wisedome, some sensualitie, some the desyre of the fleshe, is not subiect to the lawe of GOD. And although there is no condemnation for theim that beleue, and are baptized, yet the Apostle doeth confesse, that concupiscence, and lust hath of it self the nature of sinne.

the desyre of the fleshe) is not subiect to the lawe of God. And although there is no condemnation for them that beleue and are baptized: yet the Apostle doth confesse that concupiscence and luste hath of it selfe the nature of synne.

IX
Of free wille
We haue no power to dooe good woorkes pleasaunte, and acceptable to God, with out the Grace of God by Christ, preuenting us that wee maie haue a good wille, and working in us, when we haue that wille.

X.
Of free wyll.
The condition of man after the fall of Adam is suche, that he can not turne and prepare hym selfe by his owne naturall strength and good workes, to fayth and calling vpon God: Wherefore we haue no power to do good workes pleasaunt and acceptable to God, without the grace of God by Christe preuentyng us, that we may haue a good wyll, and workyng with vs, when we haue that good wyll.

X
Of Grace
The Grace of Christ, or the holie Ghost by him geuen dothe take awaie the stonie harte, and geueth an harte of fleshe. And although, those that haue no will to good thinges, he maketh them to wil, and those that would euil thinges, he maketh them not to wille the same: Yet neuerthelesse he enforceth not the wil. And therfore no man when he sinneth can excuse himself, as not worthie to be blamed or condemned. by alleging that he sinned unwillinglie, or by compulsion.

XI
Of the Justification of manne
Justification by onely faith in Jesus Christ in that sence, as it is declared

XI
Of the iustification of man.
We are accompted righteous before God, only for the merite of our Lord

in the homelie of Justification, is a moste certeine, and holesome doctrine for Christien menne.

and sauiour Jesus Christe, by faith, and not for our owne workes or deseruynges. Wherefore, that we are iustified by fayth onely, is a most wholesome doctrine, and very full of comfort, as more largely is expressed in the Homilie of iustification.

XII
Of good workes.

Albeit that good workes, which are the fruites of fayth, and folowe after iustification, can not put away our sinnes, and endure the seueritie of Gods iudgement: yet are they pleasing and acceptable to God in Christe, and do spring out necessarily of a true and liuely fayth, in so muche that by them, a lyuely fayth may be as euidently knowen, as a tree discerned by the fruit.

XII
Workes before Justification

Workes done before the Grace of Christe and the inspiratione of his spirite are not pleasaunt to GOD, forasmoche as thei spring not of Faithe in Jesu Christe, neither do thei make menne mete to receiue Grace, or (as the Schole aucthoures saie) deserue Grace of congruitie: but because thei are not done as god hath willed and commaunded theim to bee done, we doubt not, but thei haue the nature of sinne.

XIII
Of workes before iustification.

Workes done before the grace of Christe, and the inspiration of his spirite, are not pleasaunt to God, forasmuche as they spring not of fayth in Jesu Christ, neither do they make men meete to receaue grace, or (as the schole aucthours saye) deserue grace of congruitie: yea rather for that they are not done as GOD hath wylled and commaunded them to be done, we doubt not but they haue the nature of synne.

XIII
Woorkes of Supererogation

Voluntarie woorkes besides, ouer, and aboue Goddes commaundementes, whiche thei cal woorkes of Supererogation, cannot be taught without arrogancie, and iniquitie. For by theim menne dooe declare, that thei dooe not onely rendre to GOD, asmoche as thei are bounde to dooe, but that thei dooe more for his sake, then of bounden duetie is required: Whereas Christe saieth plainelie: when you haue dooen al that are commaunded you, saie, we be unprofitable seruauntes.

XIV
No man is without sinne, but Christe alone

Christe in the trueth of our nature was made like unto us in al thinges, sinne onely except, from whiche he was clearelie uoide bothe in his Fleshe, and in his Spirite. He came to be the lambe without spotte, who by Sacrifice of himself made ones for euer, should take away the sinnes of the worlde: and sinne (as Saint Jhon saieth) was not in him. But the rest, yea, althoughe we be baptized, and borne againe in Christe, yeat we all offende in many thinges: and if we saie, we haue no Sinne, wee deceiue our selues, and the trueth is not in us.

XV
Of sinne against the holie Ghoste

Euery deadlie sinne willinglie committed after Baptisme, is not Sinne against the holie Ghost, and unpardonable: wherfore the place for penitentes, is not to bee denied to soche as fall into sinne after Baptisme. After we haue receiued the holie Ghoste, we maie departe from grace geuen, and fall into sinne, and by the grace of GOD wee maie rise

XIV
Of workes of supererogation.

Voluntarie workes besydes, ouer and aboue Gods commaundementes, which they call workes of supererogation, can not be taught without arrogancie and impietie. For by them men do declare that they do not onely render vnto God as muche as they are bounde to do, but that they do more for his sake then of bounden duetie is required: Wheras Christe sayth playnly, When ye haue done al that are commaunded to you, say, We be vnprofitable seruantes.

XV
Of Christe alone without sinne.

Christe in the trueth of our nature, was made lyke vnto vs in al thinges (sinne only except) from which he was clearley voyde, both in his fleshe, and in his spirite. He came to be the lambe without spot, who by the sacrifice of hym self once made, shoulde take away the sinnes of the worlde: and sinne, (as S. John sayeth) was not in hym. But al we the rest, (although baptized, and borne agayne in Christe) yet offende in many thinges, and if we say we haue no sinne, we deceaue our selues, and the trueth is not is vs.

XVI
Of sinne after Baptisme.

Not euery deadly sinne willingly committed after baptisme, is sinne agaynst the holy ghost, and vnpardonable. Wherefore, the graunt of repentaunce is not to be denyed to such as fal into sinne after baptisme. After we haue receaued the holy ghost, we may depart from grace geuen, and fall into sinne, and by the grace of God (we may) aryse agayne again, and amende our liues. And therefore thei are to be condemned, whiche saie, thei can nomore Sinne as long as thei live here, or denie the place for penitentes to soche as truelie repent, and amende their liues.

and amend our lyues. And therefore, they are to be condemned, whiche say they can no more sinne as long as they lyue here, or denie the place of forgeuenesse to such as truely repent.

XVI
Blasphemie against the holie Ghoste.

Blasphemie against the holie Ghost is, when a man of malice and stubburnesse of minde, doeth raile upon the trueth of goddes word manifestlie perceiued, and being enemie therunto persecuteth the same. And because soche be guilty of Goddes curse, thei entangle them-selues with a moste grieuous, and hainous crime, wherupon this kinde of sinne is called and affirmed of the Lorde, vnpardonable.

XVII
Of predestination, and Election

Predestination to life, is the euerlasting purpose of God, whereby (before the foundacions of the worlde were laied) he hath constantlie decreed by his owne Judgemente screte to vs, to deliuer from curse, and damnation those whom he hath chosen out of mankinde, and to bring them to euerlasting saluation by Christ, as vesselles made to honour: whereupon, soche as haue so excellent a benefite of GOD geuen unto theim be called, according to Goddes purpose, by his spirite, woorking in due seasone, thei through grace obeie the calling, thei be justified frely, thei be made sonnes by adoptione, thei bee made like the image of Goddes onely begotten sonne Jesu Christe, thei walke religiouslie in goode woorkes, and at length by Goddes mercie, thei atteine to euerlasting felicitie.

XVII
Of predestination and election.

Predestination to lyfe, is the euerlastyng purpose of God, whereby (before the foundations of the world were layd) he hath constantly decreed by his councell secrete to vs, to deliuer from curse and damnation, those whom he hath chosen in Christe out of mankynde, and to bryng them by Christe to euerlastyng saluation, as vessels made to honour. Wherefore they which be indued with so excellent a benefite of God, be called accordyng to Gods purpose by his spirite workyng in due season: they through grace obey the callyng: they be iustified freely: they be made sonnes of God by adoption: they be made lyke the image of his onelye begotten sonne Jesus Christe: they walke religiously in good workes, and at length by gods mercy, they attaine to euerlastyng felicitie.

As the Godlie consideration of

Predestination, and our election in Christe is ful of swete, pleasaunte, and vnspeakable coumfort to Godlie persones, and soche as feele in themselues the woorking of the spirite of Christi, mortifyng the workes of the flesh, and their earthlie membres, and drawing vp their minde to high, and heauenly thinges, aswel because it doeth greatly stablish and confirme their faith of eternal Saluation to bee enioied through Christe, as because it dooeth feruentlie kindle their loue towardes Godde: So for curious and carnall persones lacking the Spirite of Christ, to haue continuallie before their yies the sentence of Goddes predestination, is a moste daungerous dounefall, whereby the Deuill maie thrust them either into desperation, or into a rechielesnesse of most vncleane liuing, no lesse perilous then desperation.

Furthermore, although the Decrees of predestination are vnknowen vnto vs, yeat we must receiue Goddes promises, in soche wise, as thei bee generallie setfoorth to vs in holie Scripture, and in our doinges that wille of Goode is to be folowed, whiche we haue expresselie declared vnto vs in the woorde of Godde.

As the godly consyderation of predestination, and our election in Christe, is full of sweete, pleasaunt, and vnspeakeable comfort to godly persons, and such as feele in them selues the working of the spirite of Christe, mortifiing the workes of the fleshe, and their earthlye members, and drawing vp their mynde to hygh and heauenly thinges, aswell because it doth greatly establyshe and confirme their fayth of eternal saluation to be enioyed through Christ, as because it doth feruently kindle their loue towardes God: So, for curious and carnal persons, lacking the spirite of Christe, to haue continually before their eyes the sentence of Gods predestination, is a most daungerous downefall, whereby the deuyll doth thrust them either into desperation, or into recheles-nesse of most vncleane liuing, no lesse perilous then desperation.

Furthermore, we must receaue Gods promises in such wyse, as they be generally set foorth to vs in holy scripture: and in our doynges, that wyl of God is to be folowed, which we haue expreslye declared vnto vs in the worde of God.

XVIII
Wee must truste to obteine eternal Saluation onely by the name of Christe.
Thei also are to be had accursed, and adhorred that presume to saie, that euery man shalbe saued by the Lawe, or secte whiche he professeth, so that he bee diligente to frame his life according to that Lawe, and the lighte of Nature: For holie Scripture doeth sette out vnto vs onely the

XVIII
Of obtaynyng eternall saluation, only by the name of Christe.
They also are to be had accursed, that presume to say, that euery man shal be saued by the lawe or sect which he professeth, so that he be diligent to frame his lyfe accordyng to that lawe, and the light of nature. For holy scripture doth set out vnto vs onely the name of Jesus Christe, whereby men must be saued.

name of Jesu Christ, wherby menne
must be saued.

XIX
All men are bounde to kepe the moral commaundementes of the Lawe
The Lawe, whiche was geuen of
GOD by Moses, although it binde
not Christian menne, as concerning
the Ceremonies, and Rites of the
same: Neither is it required, that the
Ciuile Preceptes and Ordres of it
shoulde of necessitie bee receiued in
any commune weale: Yet no Manne,
(bee he neuer so perfeicte a Christian)
is exempte and lose from the Obedience
of those Commaundementes, whiche
are called Moral: wherfore thei are
not to be harkened vnto, who affirme
that holie Scripture is geuen onlie to
the weake, and do boaste theimselues
continually of the spirit, of whom
(thei sai) thei haue learned soche
thinges as thei teache, although
thesame be most euidently repugnaunt to the holie Scripture.

XX
Of the Church
The visible Churche of Christ, is a
congregation of faiethfull Menne, in
the whiche the pure worde of God is
preached, and the sacramentes be
duelie ministred, according to
Christes ordinaunce, in all those
thinges that of necessitie are requisite
to the same.

As the Churche of Jerusalem, of
Alexandria, and of Antioche hath
erred: So also the Churche of Rome
hath erred, not onely in their liuing,
but also in matiers of their faith.

XXI
Of the aucthoritie of the Churche
It is not lawefulle for the Churche, to
ordein any thing, that is contrarie to

XIX
Of the Church.
The visible Church of Christe, is a
congregation of faythfull men, in the
which the pure worde of God is
preached, and the Sacramentes be
duely ministred, accordyng to
Christes ordinaunce in all those
thynges that of necessitie are requisite
to the same.

As the Church of Hierusalem,
Alexandria, and Antioche haue
erred: so also the Church of Rome
hath erred, not only in their liuing
and maner of ceremonies, but also in
matters of fayth.

XX
Of the aucthoritie of the Church.
The Church hath power to decree
Rites or Ceremonies, and aucthoritie

Goddes worde writen, neither maie it so expoune one place of scripture, that it be repugnaunt to an other. wherfore although the churche be a witnesse and a keper of holie writte, yet as it ought not to decree any thing againste the same: so besides the same ought it not to enforce any thing to bee beleued for necessitie of Saluation.

in controuersies of fayth: And yet it is not lawfull for the Church to ordayne any thyng that is contrarie to Gods worde written, neyther may it so expounde one place of scripture, that it be repugnaunt to another. Wherefore, although the Churche be a witnesse and a keper of holy writ: yet, as it ought not to decree any thing agaynst the same, so besides the same, ought it not to enforce any thing to be beleued for necessitie of saluation.

XXII
Of the aucthoritie of general Counsailes

Generall counsailes maie not be gathered together, without the commaundemente, and will of Princes: and when thei be gathered (forasmoche as thei be an assemblie of men wherof all be not gouerned with the spirite, and woorde of GOD) thei maie erre, and sometime haue erred, not onely in worldlie matiers, but also in thinges perteining unto God. Wherefore thinges ordeined by theim, as necessarie to Saluation, haue neither strength, nor aucthoritie, onlesse it maie be declared, that thei be taken out of holie scripture.

XXI
Of the aucthoritie of generall Counselles.

Generall Counsels may not be gathered together without the commaundement and wyll of princes. And when they be gathered together (forasmuche as they be an assemblie of men, wherof all be not gouerned with the spirite and word of God) they may erre, and sometyme haue erred, euen in thinges parteynyng vnto God. Wherfore, things ordayned by them as necessary to saluation, haue neyther strength nor aucthoritie, vnlesse it may be declared that they be taken out of holy Scripture.

XXIII
Of Purgatorie

The doctrine of Scholeaucthoures concerning purgatorie, Pardones, Worshipping, and adoration aswell of Images, as of reliques, and also inuocation of Sainctes, is a fonde thing vainlie feigned, and grounded vpon no warraunt of scripture, but rather repugnant to the woorde of God.

XXII
Of Purgatorie.

The Romishe doctrine concernyng purgatorie, pardons, worshipping and adoration as well of images, as of reliques, and also inuocation of Saintes, is a fonde thing, vainly inuented, and grounded vpon no warrantie of Scripture, but rather repugnaunt to the worde of God.

XXIV
No manne maie minister in the Congregation, except he be called.

It is not lawful for any man to take

XXIII
Of ministryng in the congregation.

It is not lawful for any man to take

vpon him the office of Publique preaching, or ministring the sacramentes in the congregation, before he be lawfullie called, and sent to execute the same. And those we ought to iudge lawfullie called, and sent, whiche be chosen, and called to this woorke by menne, who haue publique auctoritie geuen vnto them in the congregation, to cal, and sende ministres into the Lordes vineyarde.

XXV
Menne must speake in the Congregation in soche toung, as the people vnderstandeth.
It is moste semelie, and moste agreable to the woorde of God, that in the congregation nothing be openlie readde, or spoken in a toungue vnknowen to the people, the whiche thing S. Paule didde forbidde, except some were presente that should declare the same.

XXVI
Of the Sacramentes
Our LORDE Jesus Christe hathe knitte toguether a companie of newe people with Sacramentes, moste fewe in numbre, moste easie to bee kepte, moste excellent in significatione, as is Baptisme, and the Lordes Supper.

The Sacramentes were not ordeined of Christe to be gased vpon, or to be caried about, but that we shoulde rightlie use them. And in soche onely, as worthelie receiue thesame, thei haue an wholesome effecte, and operacione, and yet notthat of the woorke wrought, as some men speake, whiche worde, as it is straunge, and vnknowen to holie Scripture: So it engendreth no Godlie, but a verie supersticious sense. But thei that receiue the Sacramentes vnwoorthelie, purchace to theimselues Damnatione, as

vpon hym the office of publique preachyng, or ministring the Sacramentes in the congregation, before he be lawfully called and sent to execute the same. And those we ought to iudge lawfully called and sent, whiche be chosen and called to this worke by men who haue publique aucthoritie geuen vnto them in the congregation, to call and sende ministers into the Lordes vineyarde.

XXIV
Of speakyng in the congregation, in such a tongue as the people vnderstandeth.
It is a thing playnely repugnaunt to the worde of God, and the custome of the primitiue Churche, to haue publique prayer in the Churche, or to minister the Sacramentes in a tongue not vnderstanded of the people.

XXV
Of the Sacramentes.
Sacramentes ordayned of Christe, be not onely badges or tokens of Christian mens profession: but rather they be certaine sure witnesses and effectuall signes of grace and Gods good wyll towardes vs, by the which he doth worke inuisiblie in vs, and doth not only quicken, but also strengthen and confirme our fayth in hym.

There are two Sacramentes ordayned of Christe our Lorde in the Gospell, that is to say, Baptisme, and the Supper of the Lorde.

Those fyue, commonly called Sacramentes, that is to say, Confirmation, Penaunce, Orders, Matrimonie, and extreme Vnction, are not to be compted for Sacramentes of the gospel, being such as haue growen partly of the corrupt folowing of the Apostles, partly are states of life

Saincte Paule saieth.

Sacramentes ordeined by the worde of God be not onely Badges, and tokens of Christien Mennes professione, but rather thei bee certeine sure witnesses, and effectuall signes of grace, and Goddes good will towarde vs, by the whiche he dothe worke inuisible in vs, and dothe not onlie quicken, but also strengthen, and confirme our faith in him.

alowed in the scriptures: but yet haue not lyke nature of Sacramentes with Baptisme and the Lordes Supper, for that they haue not any visible signe or ceremonie ordayned of God.

The Sacramentes were not ordayned of Christ to be gased vpon, or to be caryed about: but that we should duely use them. And in such only, as worthyly receaue the same, they haue a wholesome effect or operation: But they that receaue them vnworthyly, purchase to them selues damnation, as S. Paul sayth.

XXVII
The wickednesse of the Ministres dooeth not take awaie the effectuall operation of Goddes ordinances.

Although in the visible Churche the euill be euer mingled with the good, and sometime the euil haue chief aucthoritie in the ministration of the worde and Sacramentes: Yet forasmoche as thei doe not thesame in their owne name, but dooe minister by Christes commission, and auctoritie: we maie use their ministerie bothe in hearing the worde of God, and in the receiuing the sacramentes, neither is the effecte of Goddes Ordinaunces taken awaie by their Wickednesse, or the grace of Goddes giftes diminished from soche, as by faieth and rightlie receiue the Sacramentes ministred vnto them, whiche bee effectuall, because of Christes institutione and promise, although thei be ministred by euil men. Neuerthelesse it apperteineth to the discipline of the Churche, that enquirie be made of soche, and that thei bee accused by those that haue knowelege of their offences, and finally being founde guiltie by iust iudgement, be deposed.

XXVI
Of the vnworthynesse of the ministers, which hinder not the effect of the Sacramentes.

Although in the visible Churche the euyl be euer myngled with the good, and sometime the euyll haue cheefe aucthoritie in the ministration of the worde and Sacramentes: yet forasmuch as they do not the same in their owne name but in Christes, and do minister by his commission and aucthoritie, we may vse their ministrie, both in hearing the word of God, and in the receauing of the Sacramentes. Neither is ye effecte of Christes ordinaunce taken away by their wickednesse, nor the grace of Gods gyftes diminished from such as by fayth and ryghtly do receaue the Sacramentes ministered vnto them, which be effectuall, because of Christes insitution and promise, although they be ministred by euyll men.

Neuerthelesse, it apparteyneth to the discipline of the Churche, that enquirie be made of euyl ministers, and that they be accused by those that haue knowledge of their offences: and finally beyng founde gyltie by iust iudgement, be deposed.

XXVIII
Of Baptisme

Baptisme is not onelie a signe of profession, and marke of difference, wherby Christien menne are discerned from other that bee not Christened, but it is also a signe, and seale of our newe birth, whereby, as by an instrument thei that receiue Baptisme rightlie, are grafted in the Churche, the promises of forgeuenesse of Sinne, and our Adoption to bee the sonnes of God, are visiblie signed and sealed, faith is confirmed, and grace increased by vertue of praier vnto God. The custome of the Churche to Christen yonge children, is to bee commended, and in any wise to bee reteined in the Churche.

XXIX
Of the Lordes Supper.

The Supper of the Lorde is not onely a signe of the loue that Christiens ought to haue among theim selues one to another, but rather it is a sacrament of our redemption by Christes death, insomoche that to soche as rightlie, woorthlelie, and with faieth receiue the same, the breade whiche we breake, is a communion of the bodie of Christe. Likewise the Cuppe of blessing, is a Communion of the bloude of Christe.

Transubstanciation, or the chaunge of the substaunce of breade, and wine into the substaunce of Christes bodie, and bloude cannot bee proued by holie writte, but is repugnaunt to the plaine woordes of Scripture, and hath geuen occasion to many supersticions.

Forasmoche as the trueth of mannes nature requireth, that the bodie of one, and theself same manne cannot be at one time in diuerse places, but must nedes be in some one certeine

XXVII
Of Baptisme.

Baptisme is not only a signe of profession, and marke of difference, whereby Christian men are discerned from other that be not christened: but is also a signe of regeneration or newe byrth, whereby as by an instrument, they that receaue baptisme rightly, are grafted into the Church: the promises of the forgeuenesse of sinne, and of our adoption to be the sonnes of God, by the holy ghost, are visibly signed and sealed: fayth is confyrmed: and grace increased by vertue of prayer vnto God. The baptisme of young children, is in any wyse to be retayned in the Churche, as most agreable with the institution of Christe.

XXVIII
Of the Lordes Supper.

The Supper of the Lord, is not only a signe of the loue that Christians ought to haue among them selues one to another: but rather it is a Sacrament of our redemption by Christes death. Insomuch that to suche as ryghtlie, worthyly, and with fayth receaue the same the bread whiche we breake is a parttakyng of the body of Christe, and likewyse the cuppe of blessing, is a parttakyng of the blood of Christe.

Transubstantiation (or the chaunge of the substaunce of bread and wine) in the Supper of the Lorde, can not be proued by holye writ, but is repugnaunt to the playne wordes of scripture, ouerthroweth the nature of a Sacrament, and hath geuen occasion to many superstitions.

The body of Christe is geuen, taken, and eaten in the Supper only after an heauenly and spirituall maner: And the meane whereby the body of Christe is receaued and eaten place: Therefore the bodie of Christe cannot bee presente at one time in many, and diuerse places. And because (as holie Scripture doeth teache) Christe was taken vp into heauen, and there shall continue vnto thende of the worlde, a faithful man ought not, either to beleue, or openlie to confesse the reall, and bodilie presence (as thei terme it) of Christes fleshe, and bloude, in the Sacramente of the Lordes supper.

The Sacramente of the Lordes supper was not commaunded by Christes ordinaunce to be kepte, caried about, lifted vp, nor worshipped.

in the Supper, is fayth.

The Sacrament of the Lordes Supper was not by Christes ordinaunce reserued, caryed about, lyfted vp, or worshipped.

XXIX
Of the wicked which do not eate the body of Christe in the vse of the Lordes Supper.

The wicked, and suche as be voyde of a liuelye fayth, although they do carnally and visibly presse with their teeth (as Saint Augustine sayth) the Sacrament of the body and blood of Christ: yet in no wyse are the partakers of Christe, but rather to their condemnation do eate and drinke the signe or Sacrament of so great a thing.

XXX
Of both kindes.

The cuppe of the Lorde is not to be denyed to the laye people. For both the partes of the Lordes Sacrament, by Christes ordinance and commaundement, ought to be ministred to all Christian men alike.

XXX
Of the perfeicte oblacion of Christe made vpon the crosse.

The offring of Christe made ones for euer, is the perfecte redemption, the

XXXI
Of the one oblation of Christe finished vppon the Crosse.

The offering of Christ once made, is the perfect redemption, propiciation, and satisfaction for all the sinnes of the whole worlde, both originall and actuall, and there is none other pacifiyng of goddes displeasure, and satisfaction for al the sinnes of the whole world, bothe original and actuall: and there is none other satisfaction for sinne, but that alone. Wherefore the sacrifices of masses, in the whiche, it was commonlie saied, that the Prieste did offre Christe for the quicke, and the dead, to haue remission of peine or sinne, were forged fables, and daungerouse deceiptes.

satisfaction for sinne, but that alone. Wherefore the sacrifices of Masses, in the which it was commonly said that the Priestes did offer Christe for the quicke and the dead, to haue remission of payne or gylt, were blasphemous fables, and daungerous deceites.

XXXI
The state of single life is commaunded to no man by the worde of God.
Bishoppes, Priestes, and Deacons are not commaunded to vowe the state of single life without mariage, neither by Goddes lawe are thei compelled to absteine from matrimonie.

XXXII
Of the mariage of Priestes.
Byshops, Priestes, and Deacons, are not commaunded by Gods lawe eyther to vowe the estate of single lyfe, or to abstayne from mariage. Therefore it is lawfull also for them, as for all other Christian men, to mary at their owne discretion, as they shall iudge the same to serue better to godlynesse.

XXXII
Excommunicate persones are to bee auoided.
That persone, whiche by open denunciacion of the Churche, is rightlie cut of from the vnitie of the Churche, and excommunicate, ought to be taken of the whole multitude of the faiethful, as an Heathen, and publicane, vntil he bee openlie reconciled by penaunce, and receiued into the Churche by a Judge that hath aucthoritie thereto.

XXXIII
Of excommunicate persons, howe they are to be auoyded.
That person whiche by open denuntiation of the Churche, is ryghtly cut of from the vnitie of the Churche, and excommunicated, ought to be taken of the whole multitude of the faythfull as an Heathen and Publicane, vntill he be openly reconciled by penaunce, and receaued into the Churche by a iudge that hath aucthoritie thereto.

XXXIII
Tradicions of the Churche
It is not necessarie that tradicions and ceremonies bee in all places one, or vtterlie like. For at al times thei haue been diuers, and maie be chaunged, according to the diuersitie of countries, and mennes maners, so that nothing bee ordeined against

XXXIV
Of the traditions of the Churche.
It is not necessarie that traditions and ceremonies be in al places one, or vtterly like, for at all times they haue ben diuerse, and may be chaunged accordyng to the diuersitie of Countreys, times, and mens maners, so that nothing be ordeyned against

goddes worde.

Whosoeuer through his priuate iudgement willinglie, and purposelie doeth openlie breake the tradicions and Ceremonies of the Churche, whiche bee not repugnaunte to the worde of God, and bee ordeined, and approued by common aucthoritie, ought to be rebuked openlie (that other maie feare to doe the like) as one that offendeth against the common ordre of the churche, and hurteth thauctoritie of the Magistrate, and woundeth the consciences of the weake brethren.

Gods worde. Whosoeuer through his priuate iudgement, wyllyngly and purposely doth openly breake the traditions and ceremonies of the Church, which be not repugnaunt to the worde of God, and be ordayned and approued by common aucthoritie, ought to be rebuked openly, (that other may feare to do the lyke) as he that offendeth agaynst the Common order of the Churche, and hurteth the aucthoritie of the Magistrate, and woundeth the consciences of the weake brethren.

Euery particuler or nationall Churche, hath aucthoritie to ordaine, chaunge, and abolishe ceremonies or rites of the Churche ordyened onlye by mans aucthoritie, so that all thinges be done to edifiyng.

XXXIV
Homelies

Thomelies of late geuen, and set out by the kinges aucthoritie, be godlie and holsome, conteining doctrine to bee receiued of all menne, and therefore are to be readde to the people diligentlie, distinctlie, and plainlie.

XXXV
Of Homilies.

The seconde booke of Homilies, the seuerall titles wherof we haue ioyned vnder this article, doth conteyne a godly and wholesome doctrine, and necessarie for these tymes, as doth the former booke of Homilies, whiche were set foorth in the time of Edwarde the sixt: and therefore we iudge them to be read in Churches by the Ministers diligently, and distinctly, that they may be vnderstanded of the people.

Of the names of the Homilies.

1 Of the right vse of the Churche.
2 Agaynst perill of Idolatrie.
3 Of repayring and keping cleane of Churches.
4 Of good workes, first of fastyng.
5 Agaynst gluttony and drunkennesse.
6 Against excesse of apparell.
7 Of prayer.
8 Of the place and time of prayer.
9 That common prayers and Sacramentes ought to be ministred in a

knowen tongue.
10 Of the reuerente estimation of Gods worde.
11 Of almes doing.
12 Of the Natiuitie of Christe.
13 Of the passion of Christe.
14 Of the resurrection of Christe.
15 Of the worthie receauing of the Sacrament of the body and blood of Christe.
16 Of the gyftes of the holy ghost.
17 For the Rogation dayes.
18 Of the state of Matrimonie.
19 Of repentaunce.
20 Agaynst Idlenesse.
21 Agaynst rebellion.

XXXV
Of the booke of Praiers and Ceremonies of the Churche of Englande.

The Booke whiche of very late time was geuen to the Churche of Englande by the kinges aucthoritie, and the Parlamente, conteining the maner and fourme of praiyng, and ministring the Sacramentes in the Churche of Englande, likewise also the booke of ordring Ministers of the Churche, set foorth by the forsaied aucthoritie, are godlie, and in no poincte repugnaunt to the holsome doctrine of the Gospel but agreable thereunto, ferthering and beautifiyng the same not a litle, and therfore of al faithfull members of the Churche of Englande, and chieflie of the ministers of the worde, thei ought to be receiued, and allowed with all readinesse of minde, and thankes geuing, and to bee commended to the people of God.

XXXVI
Of consecration of Bishops and ministers.

The booke of Consecration of Archbyshops, and Byshops, and orderyng of Priestes and Deacons, lately set foorth in the time of Edwarde the sixt, and confyrmed at the same tyme by aucthoritie of Parliament, doth conteyne all thinges necessarie to suche consecration and orderyng: neyther hath it any thing, that of it selfe is superstitious or vngodly. And therefore, whosoeuer are consecrate or ordered accordyng to the rites of that booke, sence the seconde yere of the aforenamed king Edwarde, vnto this time, or hereafter shalbe consecrated or ordered accordyng to the same rites, we decree all such to be ryghtly, orderly, and lawfully consecrated and ordered.

XXXVI
Of Ciuile magistrates

The king of Englande is Supreme head in earth, nexte vnder Christe, of the Churche of Englande, and Jrelande.

The Bishoppe of Rome hath no iurisdiction in this Realme of Englande.

The ciuile Magistrate is ordeined, and allowed of God : wherefore we must obeie him, not onely for feare of punishment, but also for conscience sake.

The ciuile lawes maie punishe Christien men with death, for heinous, and grieuous offences.

It is lawefull for Christians, at the commaundement of the Magistrate, to weare weapons, and to serue in laweful warres.

XXXVII
Of the Ciuill Magistrates.

The Queenes Maiestie hath the cheefe power in this Realme of Englande, and other her dominions, vnto whom the cheefe gouernment of all estates of this Realme, whether they be Ecclesiasticall or Ciuile, in all causes doth apparteine, and is not, nor ought to be subiect to any forraigne iurisdiction.

Where we attribute to the Queenes Maiestie the cheefe gouernment, by whiche titles we vnderstande the mindes of some slaunderous folkes to be offended: we geue not to our princes the ministring either of God's word, or of Sacraments, the which thing the Iniunctions also lately set forth by Elizabeth our Queene, doth most plainlie testifie: But that only prerogatiue whiche we see to haue ben geuen alwayes to all godly Princes in holy Scriptures by God him selfe, that is, that they should rule all estates and degrees committed to their charge by God, whether they be Ecclesiasticall or Temporall, and restraine with the ciuill sworde the stubberne and euyll doers.

The bishop of Rome hath iurisdiction in this Realme of Englande.

The lawes of the Realme may punishe Christian men with death, for heynous and greeuous offences.

It is lawfull for Christian men, at the commaundement of the Magistrate, to weare weapons, and serue in the warres.

XXXVII
Christien mennes goddes are not commune.

The richesse and gooddes of christians are not commune, as touching the right title and possession of the same (as certain anabaptistes dooe falslie boaste); notwithstanding euery man ought of such thinges as he possesseth, liberallie to geue almes to the pore, according to his habilitie.

XXXVIII
Of Christian mens goodes, which are not common.

The ryches and goodes of Christians are not common, as touching the ryght, title, and possession of the same, as certayne Anabaptistes do falsely boast. Notwithstandyng euery man ought of suche thinges as he possesseth, liberally to geue almes to the poore, accordyng to his habilitie.

XXXVIII
Christien menne maie take an Othe

As we confesse that vaine, and rashe swearing is forbed Christien men by our Lorde Iesu Christ, and his Apostle Iames: so we iudge that christien religion doeth not prohibite, but that a man maie sweare, when the magistrate requireth in a cause of faith, and charitie, so it bee doen (according to the Prophetes teaching) in iustice, iudgemente, and trueth.

XXXIX
Of a Christian mans othe.

As we confesse that vayne and rashe swearing is forbidden Christian men by our lord Iesus Christe, and Iames his Apostle: So we iudge that Christian religion doth not prohibite, but that a man may sweare when the Magistrate requireth, in a cause of faith and charitie, so it be done accordyng to the prophetes teaching, in iustice, iudgement, and trueth.

XXXIX
The Resurrection of the dead is not yeat brought to passe.

The Resurrection of the dead is not as yet brought to passe, as though it only belonged to the soulle, whiche by the grace of Christe is raised from the death of sinne, but it is to be loked for at the laste daie: for then (as Scripture doeth moste manifestlie testifie) to all that bee dead their awne bodies, fleshe, and bone shalbe

restored, that the whole man maie
(according to his workes) haue other
rewarde, or punishment, as he hath
liued vertuouslie, or wickedlie.

XL
*The soulles of them that departe this
life doe neither die with the bodies,
nor sleep idlie.*

Thei whiche saie, that the soulles of
suche as departe hens doe sleepe,
being without al sence, fealing, or
perceiuing, vntil the daie of
iudgement, or affirme that the soulles
die with the bodies, and at the laste
daie shalbe raised vp with thesame,
doe vtterlie dissent from the right
beliefe declared to vs in holie
Scripture.

XLI
Heretickes called Millenarii.
Thei that goe about to renewe the
fable of heretickes called Millenarii,
be repugnant to holie Scripture, and
caste them selues headlong into a
Juishe dotage.

XLII
*All men shall not bee saued at the
length*
Thei also are worthie of condem-
nacion, who indeuoure at this time to
restore the dangerouse opinion, that
al menne, be thei neuer so vngodlie,
shall at length bee saued, when thei
haue suffered paines for their sinnes a
certaine time appoincted by Goddes
iustice.

Appendix 2

THE WESTMINSTER CONFESSION OF FAITH (1647)

THE WESTMINSTER CONFESSION OF FAITH (1647)

Chapter III: Of Gods eternall Decree

God from all eternity did, by the most wise and holy Counsell of his own Will, freely and unchangeably ordain whatsoever comes to passe: yet so, as thereby neither is God the Author of sin, nor is violence offered to the will of the Creatures, nor is the Liberty or contingency of second Causes taken away, but rather established.

II   Although God knowes whatsoever may, or can come to passe upon all supposed conditions, yet hath he not decreed any thing because he foresaw it as future, or as that which would come to passe upon such conditions.

III   By the decree of God, for the manifestation of his Glory, some men and Angels are predestinated unto everlasting life, and others fore-ordained to everlasting death.

IV   These angels and men thus predestinated and fore-ordained, are particularly and unchangeably designed: and their number is so certain, and definite, that it can not be either increased, or diminished.

V   Those of man-kinde that are predestinated unto Life, God, before the foundation of the world was laid according to his eternall and immutable purpose, and the secret counsell and good pleasure of his Will, hath chosen, in Christ, unto everlasting glory, out of his meer free grace and love, without any foresight of Faith, or good works, or perseverance in either of them, or any other thing in the creature, as conditions, or causes moving him thereunto, and all to the praise of his glorious grace.

VI   As God hath appointed the Elect unto glory, so hath he, by the eternall and most free purpose of his Will, foreordained all the meanes thereunto. Wherefore they who are elected, being fallen in *Adam*, are redeemed by Christ, are effectually called unto faith in Christ, by his Spirit working in due season, are justified, adopted, sanctified, and kept by his power through faith unto salvation. Neither are any other redeemed by Christ, effectually called, justified, adopted, sanctified and saved, but the Elect onely.

VII   The rest of man-kinde God was pleased, according to the unsearchable counsell of his own Will, whereby he extendeth or with-holdeth mercy, as he pleaseth, for the glory of his Soveraign Power over his creatures, to passe by: and to Ordain them to dishonour and wrath, for their sin, to the praise of his glorious justice.

VIII The doctrine of this high Mystery of Predestination is to be handled with speciall prudence and care, that men attending the will of God revealed in his Word, and yeelding obedience thereunto, may, from the certainty of their effectuall Vocation, be assured of their eternall Election. So shall this Doctrine afford matter of praise, reverence, and admiration of God, and of humility, diligence, and abundant consolation to all that sincerely obey the Gospel.

Chapter XXV: Of the Church

The Catholick or Vniversall Church which is invisible, consists of the whole number of the Elect, that have bin, are, or shall be gathered into one, under Christ the Head thereof; and is, the Spouse, the Body, the fullnesse of Him that filleth all in all.

II   The visible Church, which is also Catholick or Vniversall, under the Gospell (not confined to one Nation, as before, under the Law) consists of all those, throughout the World, that professe the true Religion; and of their children; and is, the Kingdome of the Lord Iesus Christ, the House and Family of God, out of which there is no ordinary possibility of Salvation.

III   Vnto this Catholick Visible Church, Christ hath given the Ministery, Oracles, and Ordinances of God, for the gathering, and perfecting of the Saints, in this life, to the end of the world: and doth by his own presence and Spirit, according to his promise, make them effectuall thereunto.

IV   This Catholick Church hath bin sometimes more, sometimes lesse visible. And particular Churches which are Members thereof, are more or lesse pure, according as the Doctrine of the Gospel is taught and imbraced, Ordinances administred, and publick worship performed more or less purely in them.

V   The purest Churches under Heaven are subject both to mixture, and errour; and some have so degenerated, as to become no Churches of Christ, but synagogues of Satan. Neverthelesse, there shall be alwayes a Church on Earth, to Worship God according to his will.

VI   There is no other Head of the Church, but the Lord Iesus Christ: Nor can the Pope of Rome, in any sence be head thereof; but is, that Antichrist, that man of sin, and Sun of Perdition, that exalteth himself, in the Church against Christ, and all that is called God.